"This book on the final judgment of (expect from the scholarship of Tom Sc fidelity, practical application, and clear writing. The topic is not an easy one to write on, but it is a necessary one lest we forget why the gospel of Jesus is indeed good news."

Jonny Gibson, Associate Professor of Old Testament, Westminster Theological Seminary; coeditor, *Ruined Sinners to Reclaim*

"This is an important study of a biblical truth that needs to be proclaimed to our generation. Tom Schreiner shows that God's final judgment is based on his perfect goodness that deals righteously with human sin to establish his righteousness in the world. The book handles the different sections of the Bible carefully and thoroughly, highlighting and discussing important themes, and painting a powerful picture in the mind of his reader."

John Coulson, Deputy Principal and Lecturer in Bible, Brisbane School of Theology

"Does it sound uplifting to read an entire book on what the Bible teaches about God's judgment? It should. In this book, Tom Schreiner delivers to us the hard truth about God's righteous judgment that we deserve for our sinful condition. The bad news is really bad. But that is what makes the good news about God's merciful kindness in Jesus the Messiah so uplifting. The more accurately you understand God's righteous judgment, the more brightly God's saving work shines."

Andy Naselli, Professor of Systematic Theology and New Testament, Bethlehem College and Seminary; Elder, The North Church, Mounds View, Minnesota

"This is a deeply insightful book on an important, oft-overlooked, and confronting truth. It can be painful to consider our sin and God's judgment, but doing so helps us appreciate the grace of God more deeply. Tom Schreiner has written a penetrating, accessible guide to this important topic."

Peter Orr, Lecturer in New Testament, Moore Theological College

The Justice and Goodness of God

The Justice and Goodness of God

A Biblical Case for the Final Judgment

Thomas R. Schreiner

WHEATON, ILLINOIS

The Justice and Goodness of God: A Biblical Case for the Final Judgment
© 2024 by Thomas R. Schreiner
Published by Crossway
      1300 Crescent Street
      Wheaton, Illinois 60187

Cover design: Jordan Singer

First printing 2024

Printed in the United States of America

Unless otherwise indicated, Scripture quotations are from the ESV® Bible (The Holy Bible, English Standard Version®), © 2001 by Crossway, a publishing ministry of Good News Publishers. Used by permission. All rights reserved. The ESV text may not be quoted in any publication made available to the public by a Creative Commons license. The ESV may not be translated into any other language.

Scripture quotations marked NIV are taken from the Holy Bible, New International Version®, NIV®. Copyright © 1973, 1978, 1984, 2011 by Biblica, Inc.™ Used by permission of Zondervan. All rights reserved worldwide. www.zondervan.com. The "NIV" and "New International Version" are trademarks registered in the United States Patent and Trademark Office by Biblica, Inc.™

All emphases in Scripture quotations have been added by the author.

Trade paperback ISBN: 978-1-4335-9119-8
ePub ISBN: 978-1-4335-9121-1
PDF ISBN: 978-1-4335-9120-4

Library of Congress Cataloging-in-Publication Data

Names: Schreiner, Thomas R., author.
Title: The justice and goodness of God : a Biblical case for the final judgment / Thomas R. Schreiner.
Description: Wheaton, Illinois : Crossway, 2024. | Includes bibliographical references and index.
Identifiers: LCCN 2023027178 (print) | LCCN 2023027179 (ebook) | ISBN 9781433591198 (trade paperback) |
    ISBN 9781433591204 (pdf) | ISBN 9781433591211 (epub)
Subjects: LCSH: Judgment of God. | God (Christianity)—Goodness.
Classification: LCC BT180.J8 S38 2024 (print) | LCC BT180.J8 (ebook) | DDC 231/.8—dc23/eng/20240110
LC record available at https://lccn.loc.gov/2023027178
LC ebook record available at https://lccn.loc.gov/2023027179

Crossway is a publishing ministry of Good News Publishers.

BP			33	32	31	30	29	28	27	26	25	24
15	14	13	12	11	10	9	8	7	6	5	4	3	2	1

Contents

Preface

WHY WOULD ANYONE want to write on the final judgment? It might seem that anyone who writes on this theme is obsessed with the negative, with hate instead of love, with punishment instead of mercy, with crankiness instead of joy. It is probably true that some who focus on judgment live in winter instead of summer and have acerbic personalities, and maybe some readers will suspect that I am of the same temperament. In any case, let me explain why I wanted to write a book on the final judgment.

First, Scripture often talks about judgment; it is a pervasive theme in both the Old Testament and the New Testament, though I limit myself mainly to the New Testament since the topic is far too large to include the whole Bible in a brief book. Judgment isn't the invention of unhappy people but represents the truth. Adolf Schlatter rightly says, "When truth becomes our judge and shows us what is reprehensible, we fall silent before our just Judge."[1]

Second, judgment is often ignored or overlooked in scholarship in that there are not many books on the theme. Still, some helpful treatments are available,[2] but my intention is to write a brief and accessible

---

1   Adolf Schlatter, *Do We Know Jesus? Daily Insights for the Mind and Soul,* trans. Andreas J. Köstenberger and Robert W. Yarbrough (Grand Rapids, MI: Kregel, 2005), 51.

2   R. V. G. Tasker, *The Biblical Doctrine of the Wrath of God* (London: Tyndale Press, 1951); Leon Morris, *The Biblical Doctrine of Judgment* (Grand Rapids, MI: Eerdmans, 1960); John R. Coulson, *The Righteous Judgment of God: Aspects of Judgment in Paul's Letters* (Eugene, OR: Wipf & Stock, 2016); Brendan Byrne, *Paul and the Economy of Salvation:*

introduction to the theme and to restrict the study mainly (though not exclusively) to the final judgment. Certainly the scriptural story can't be understood apart from the last judgment. Salvation, justification, reconciliation, redemption, regeneration, adoption, and other salvific realities don't make any sense if human beings don't deserve condemnation. If there is nothing to be saved from, we don't need to be justified, reconciled, redeemed, and forgiven.

Third, I believe one of the reasons the Christian gospel seems alien to many today is that they reject the notion of a last judgment. As Leon Morris says, the modern person "has largely dismissed the thought of final judgment from his mind. He does not think of himself as accountable. The New Testament does not share his unreasoning optimism."[3] The final destruction of sinners, of those who rebel against the Lord, of those who don't put their faith and trust in him, seems unjust and vindictive to many today. Morris again is to the point: "It seems axiomatic to us that God in love will deliver all men. This is not what Scripture teaches."[4] People aren't inclined to turn to Jesus Christ for forgiveness and to escape wrath since they don't think their sins warrant punishment. I am under no illusion that non-Christians will read this book, or that unbelievers, even if they did read it, would be persuaded. I am writing this book for missionaries, for pastors, for Christians in ministry, and for all Christians to remind us that judgment is fundamental to the message we proclaim so that we will not be ashamed of or neglect speaking about judgment. Indeed, I hope Christians will rejoice in judgment, not because they long for the punishment of others (since we pray and hope that all will be saved) but because judgment displays the holiness and goodness of God. Without judgment, God would not be good, and life on earth would be without meaning since our moral decisions would not ultimately matter. They might matter to us personally, but there would be no final reckoning for our lives,

---

   Reading from the Perspective of the Last Judgment (Grand Rapids, MI: Baker Academic, 2021).

3   Morris, *The Biblical Doctrine of Judgment*, 65–66.

4   Morris, *The Biblical Doctrine of Judgment*, 69.

no ultimate accountability for our actions, and thus no significance to our lives—and that would be bad news indeed.

I am grateful to Crossway for publishing this book and in particular for Justin Taylor who carefully read an earlier draft and made many helpful suggestions. I have noted some of what he suggested in footnotes. Finally, my friend and outstanding editor Chris Cowan proved to be an amazing help with his keen reading and many helpful suggestions.

Abbreviations

ACCS	Ancient Christian Commentary on Scripture
BBR	*Bulletin for Biblical Research*
BDAG	Danker, Frederick W., Walter Bauer, William F. Arndt, and F. Wilbur Gingrich. *Greek-English Lexicon of the New Testament and Other Early Christian Literature.* 3rd ed. Chicago: University of Chicago Press, 2000.
BECNT	Baker Exegetical Commentary on the New Testament
BSac	*Bibliotheca Sacra*
CSC	Christian Standard Commentary
2 En.	2 Enoch
2 Esd.	2 Esdras
ET	English translation
ITC	International Theological Commentary
LCC	Library of Christian Classics
4 Macc.	4 Maccabees
LXX	Septuagint
MT	Masoretic Text
NICNT	New International Commentary on the New Testament
NIDNTTE	*New International Dictionary of New Testament Theology and Exegesis.* 4 vols. Revision editor, Moisés Silva. Grand Rapids, MI: Zondervan, 2014.
NIGTC	New International Greek Testament Commentary
Sib. Or.	Sibylline Oracles

SSST   Short Studies in Systematic Theology

Them   *Themelios*

T. Isaac   Testament of Isaac

TLOT   *Theological Lexicon of the Old Testament*. 3 vols. Edited by Ernst Jenni and Claus Westermann. Translated by Mark E. Biddle. Peabody, MA: Hendrickson, 1997.

WBC   Word Biblical Commentary

WUNT   Wissenschaftliche Untersuchungen zum Neuen Testament

1

Only a Holy God

Righteous are you, O LORD,
and right are your rules.
PSALM 119:137

Introduction

Leon Morris brilliantly begins his book on judgment with several texts showing that judgment and justice belong together: if there is no judgment, then there is no justice.[1] Isaiah proclaims that "the LORD is a God of justice" (Isa. 30:18). Malachi casts aspersions on those who doubt whether God is "the God of justice" (Mal. 2:17) since no one will trust or obey the Lord if he is unjust. Isaiah reminds us that the Lord doesn't need human beings to inform him about what is just:

Who taught him the path of justice,
    and taught him knowledge,
    and showed him the way of understanding? (Isa. 40:14)

Abraham prays to the Lord about the fate of Sodom, asking with confidence, "Shall not the Judge of all the earth do what is just?" (Gen.

---

1 Leon Morris, *The Biblical Doctrine of Judgment* (Grand Rapids, MI: Eerdmans, 1960), 7–8.

18:25). The Scriptures assure us that God is fair and just since "I the LORD love justice" (Isa. 61:8).

The Lord loves justice because his very person, his very nature, is just. He doesn't love justice as something outside of himself. Thus Moses sings,

The Rock, his work is perfect,
    for all his ways are justice. (Deut. 32:4)

The psalmist declares, "Righteousness and justice are the foundation of his throne" (Ps. 97:2). The Lord's judgments are right because he loves justice, because *he is justice*.[2] He doesn't need anyone to teach him justice since it is his very nature or character—justice defines him.[3] Or, better, the Lord defines justice. Since God is just, he always does what is right, and his judgments should not be questioned but praised. Because if there were no justice in the world, the world would not make sense. It would be a place of absolute chaos and anarchy.[4]

We see God's justice from the first story in the Bible. Adam and Eve were commanded not to eat of the tree of the knowledge of good and evil (Gen. 2:17; 3:2–3), and they were threatened with death if they violated God's instructions (Gen. 2:17; 3:3). We are not given any reason why eating from the particular tree is forbidden. We can say that God as the Creator and Lord defines good and evil, determining what is right and wrong. This is not to say that good and evil are arbitrary, since moral norms reflect God's character and nature, but as the sovereign Lord of all, God may also give commands that aren't in and of

2 This fits with the notion of divine simplicity so that we don't conceive of God as made up of parts.
3 Morris says about the Lord, "He is essentially just, just in his inner being. Justice is not a matter of indifference, but one of passionate concern." Morris, *The Biblical Doctrine of Judgment*, 19.
4 As Jonathan Leeman says, "Apart from God's judgment, this universe makes no sense. Everything is worthless. Nothing is precious or valuable or worthwhile. Just ask the nihilist." Jonathan Leeman, *The Rule of Love: How the Local Church Should Reflect God's Love and Authority* (Wheaton, IL: Crossway, 2018), 122.

themselves moral norms. Adam and Eve transgressed God's command, rejecting his lordship over their lives, and consequently they were separated from God (Gen. 3:7–19), expelled from paradise (Gen. 3:23–24), and destined to die physically. Judgment for evil manifests itself in the earliest pages of the biblical story, showing that evil has consequences.

The flood story represents another shocking account of judgment, and once again it occurs at the outset of history, or at least the history that is recorded and written down. Human beings were indicted for being corrupt (Gen. 6:3, 11). Wickedness multiplied on earth like weeds spring up in a green lawn, and "every intention of the thoughts of [man's] heart was only evil continually" (Gen. 6:5). Two features of the account are rather striking.

First, the descriptions of human wickedness are vague. We are told that human beings were corrupt and wicked, that their thoughts were always evil. But a specific portrait or description of the evil they engaged in is lacking. We might expect a lurid account of what human beings were doing, given the horrific deluge that destroyed virtually the entire human race. Instead of their evil being detailed, we are invited to use our imaginations to sketch in the evils perpetrated by human beings.

Second, all except eight people in the world were swept away in the cataclysm that snuffed out their lives. If we ask ourselves why such a drastic measure was needed, the answer is that human beings were corrupt and wicked, that they practiced what was evil. In fact, we are told that every thought and motive was evil (Gen. 6:5). The judgment was drastic and overwhelming because the evil being perpetrated was comprehensive, devastating, and horrific.

The reason for such a judgment isn't obvious to many people in our own world, and thus I will attempt to chase down in this chapter the reasons for judgment in the Old Testament witness. There is no attempt to be complete here; instead I will take soundings of some Old Testament texts.[5] In addition, I am treating the Old Testament as a canonical

---

5   For the last judgment in Second Temple Jewish literature, see Brendan Byrne, *Paul and the Economy of Salvation: Reading from the Perspective of the Last Judgment* (Grand Rapids, MI: Baker Academic, 2021), 16–34.

unity, and thus the answer we are seeking must be discerned by reading the Old Testament witness as a whole. Furthermore, it is important to recognize that the judgment of the flood is a preview of the final judgment. In the New Testament, the flood has a typological relationship to the final judgment, pointing to and anticipating it. The judgment that will come at Jesus's return is compared to the judgment that devastated the world in the flood (Matt. 24:38–39; Luke 17:26–27; 2 Pet. 2:5, 9; 3:6). Thus, Old Testament accounts of judgment have an organic relationship to the final judgment, and they point to that judgment.

God Is Holy

One answer—a fundamental and important answer—as to why God judges evil is that he is holy. Often in the Old Testament, especially in Isaiah, Yahweh is called "the Holy One of Israel" (Ps. 78:41; Isa. 1:4; 5:19, 24; 10:20; 12:6; 17:7; 29:19; 30:11, 12, 15; 31:1; 37:23; 41:14, 16, 20; 43:3, 14; 45:11; 47:4; 48:17; 49:7; 54:5; 55:5; 60:9, 14; Jer. 50:29; 51:5). We often read about Yahweh's "holy name" (e.g., 1 Chron. 16:10, 35; Pss. 30:4; 33:21; 111:9; Ezek. 36:20, 21, 22; 39:7, 25; 43:7, 8; Amos 2:7), which means that holiness is the Lord's very nature and being.

Holiness is often defined as being separated from evil, though others have said that it signifies what is consecrated and devoted.[6] These two definitions may not be as far apart as we might think since what is consecrated and devoted is also separated from common use. For instance, the Holy Place and the Most Holy Place are devoted to the sacrificial cult, but we could say that both places are separated from common use as well. So, too, the Sabbath is a consecrated day, a holy day (Ex. 20:8), but it is also separated from other days and, thus, special. We could say the same thing about holy garments (Ex. 28:2), holy offerings (Ex. 28:38), holy anointing oil (Ex. 30:25), and so on. They are separated from ordinary life and consecrated for special use.

We also receive further help by investigating other words associated with holiness. For instance, priests are to distinguish "between the

---

6   Peter J. Gentry, "The Meaning of 'Holy' in the Old Testament," *BSac* 170 (2013): 400–417.

holy and the common, and between the unclean and the clean" (Lev. 10:10; cf. Ezek. 22:26; 44:23). The holy is in the same category as that which is clean, while the unholy is unclean and defiled. Those from Aaron's house can't eat holy offerings until they are clean (Lev. 22:4). These texts refer to ritual defilement, which is not necessarily equated with sinfulness. Still, it seems that the reason uncleanness exists is because of the presence of sin in the world. Uncleanness, then, doesn't necessarily point to personal sin, but it signifies a sickness in a world that is deformed and bent due to human evil. God stands apart from the world because of his holiness. "There is none holy like the LORD" (1 Sam. 2:2). Since the Lord is the "Holy One," no one can be compared to him or is equal to him (Isa. 40:25).

The Lord is uniquely holy, and there is clearly a moral dimension to holiness. When the ark was returned from the Philistines to Israel in Beth-shemesh, some looked inside the ark and seventy people were struck dead (1 Sam. 6:19). They immediately responded, "Who is able to stand before the LORD, this holy God?" (1 Sam. 6:20). The author is clearly telling us that the sin of Israel is such that they were unable to live in God's presence, since he is the Holy One—that is, he is beautiful and full of goodness in contrast to the sinfulness of human beings.

Nor is this an isolated thought. The psalmist asks,

> O LORD, who shall sojourn in your tent?
>   Who shall dwell on your holy hill? (Ps. 15:1)

The answer reveals that holiness has to do with the Lord's moral perfection and his blazing goodness, since those who can live on his holy mountain are those who live righteously, who refrain from slander, who do not injure their neighbors, who esteem the godly, who are true to their word, and who don't take interest and deprive the poor of their income (Ps. 15:2–5). A similar question is asked in Psalm 24:

> Who shall ascend the hill of the LORD?
>   And who shall stand in his holy place? (Ps. 24:3)

The answer again has to do with goodness, since access to God is restricted to those who have "clean hands" and "a pure heart" and are characterized by honesty (Ps. 24:4). It seems apparent in this context that God's holiness refers to his moral perfection and that righteousness is required of human beings as well.

Another fascinating window into God's holiness is Psalm 99, where Yahweh reigns as one "enthroned upon the cherubim" (Ps. 99:1). Given the greatness of the Lord, people are to "praise your great and awesome name," and the psalmist exclaims, "Holy is he!" (Ps. 99:3). God's holiness here is related to his transcendence, to his sovereignty, to his reign as King over all. Yahweh's holiness is a central theme of the psalm. Readers are exhorted,

> Exalt the LORD our God;
>   worship at his footstool!
>   Holy is he! (Ps. 99:5; cf. 99:9)

Still, God's holiness isn't restricted to his transcendence but is also reflected in the "decrees" and "statutes" given to Israel (Ps. 99:7 CSB). The moral dimension of his holiness is confirmed in 99:8 since God is identified as one who forgives and also as "an avenger of their wrongdoings." God's holiness is such that sin either must be forgiven or avenged; it can't be left alone because sin defaces, deforms, and destroys. God's dazzling beauty and loveliness can't allow sin to coexist with him; doing such would compromise his holiness, his very being.

Isaiah 6 is rightly famous, and it casts more light on our theme. Yahweh sits transcendently and magnificently as the King in his temple. The seraphim stand around the Lord with their six wings. They cover their faces with two wings since the Lord is ever and always the Holy One, and thus they can't look on his face. With two wings they cover their feet, which is another indication of their inferiority in the presence of the Creator and sovereign of all things. With two wings they fly as they serve at Yahweh's behest, carrying out his decrees in the world. The seraphim praise the Lord as the thrice Holy One, signifying his infinite and maximal holiness, as the one whose glory fills the entire world. Yahweh's holiness has a transcendent character because he is the King of the universe and even angels who are not defiled with sin cannot gaze at him.

The temple fills with "smoke," and the Hebrew word used in Isaiah 6:4 occurs in the text about the "smoking fire pot" that passed between the pieces in the Lord's covenant with Abram (Gen. 15:17). Mount Sinai also smoked like a furnace when the Lord descended on it (Ex. 19:18). In 2 Samuel 22:9, smoke is aligned with God's consuming fire (cf. Ps. 18:8). The temple filling with smoke communicates God's presence, and the parallels and context suggest that his presence is terrifying. It is frightening because of Yahweh's holiness, his moral perfection.

Isaiah's response supports such a reading. Isaiah pronounces a woe on himself since he is "a man of unclean lips" inasmuch as he has seen "the King, the LORD of hosts" (Isa. 6:5). We see further evidence that moral perfection characterizes Yahweh's holiness when Isaiah became painfully aware of his uncleanness, an uncleanness that needed to be atoned for before he could serve as the Lord's messenger (Isa. 6:6–7). When human beings see God as he is, reigning and ruling transcendently as King and Lord, then they realize that they can't stand in his presence since he is beautiful in holiness.

It would be misleading to link holiness only with God's judgment. Hosea 11 predicts Israel's exile to Assyria after the nation violated the Lord's covenant stipulations. Still, the judgment will not be comprehensive and complete so that the nation is entirely obliterated. The Lord will not wipe them out as he destroyed Admah and Zeboiim, on which fire rained down when Sodom and Gomorrah were annihilated (Hos. 11:8). Because the Lord is not a human being, because he is "the Holy One," he will spare his people (Hos. 11:9). God is holy in that he is true to his name; he will not violate or renege on his covenant promises to Israel. We see that God is also holy in his mercy and his love.

Yahweh is the "One who is high and lifted up," who lives "in the high and holy place" (Isa. 57:15). Surprisingly, however, the transcendent one is also immanent. He dwells with his people, with the one "who is of a contrite and lowly spirit," promising

> to revive the spirit of the lowly,
>> and to revive the heart of the contrite. (Isa. 57:15)

God's holiness doesn't mean that he isn't merciful (we just saw his mercy in Hos. 11), but we do need to think about what it means for God to show mercy.

We saw earlier in Isaiah 6 that God's holiness doesn't preclude fellowship with human beings since there is forgiveness and atonement. God's holiness should not be interpreted to mean that he doesn't show mercy. God as the Holy One has fellowship with a lowly and oppressed people. God's holiness and forgiveness need to be read in light of the larger storyline of Isaiah, since in Isaiah 53 the servant of the Lord bears and suffers for the sins of his people. He has "borne our griefs" and was "stricken, smitten by God, and afflicted" (Isa. 53:4). Isaiah emphasizes that the servant took the punishment we deserved:

> He was pierced for our transgressions;
>> he was crushed for our iniquities;
> upon him was the chastisement that brought us peace. (Isa. 53:5)

God has mercy on those who have gone astray, but not without satisfying his justice:

> the LORD has laid on him [the servant]
>> the iniquity of us all. (Isa. 53:6).

Even though he was without sin (Isa. 53:7, 9), the servant "was numbered with the transgressors" and "bore the sin of many" (Isa. 53:12). Human beings have fellowship with the Holy One of Israel because of the Lord's forgiving mercy, because the servant took upon himself the punishment sinners deserved, satisfying the justice God demanded. In the death of the servant, both the justice and love of God are displayed.

God Is Righteous

The righteousness of God is a major theme in the Old Testament.[7] Even though it is not the focus of this book, it is important to note that God's righteousness in the Old Testament is often a saving righteousness instead of a judging righteousness. (Paul picks up this theme of God's saving righteousness in Rom. 1:17 when he declares that God's saving righteousness is revealed in the gospel.) Remarkably, some scholars deny that God's righteousness is ever a judging righteousness in the Old Testament.[8] As we shall see, this assessment is clearly mistaken, even if the number of verses that forge this connection is limited.

Before linking together God's righteousness and judgment, it is imperative to remind ourselves that the Lord *is* righteous, which means that he always does what is right and virtuous. The notion is expressed well in Deuteronomy 32:4:

> The Rock, his work is perfect,
>   for all his ways are justice.
> A God of faithfulness and without iniquity,
>   just and upright is he.

The affirmations supporting God's righteousness are striking and pervasive in that his justice, faithfulness, impartiality, righteousness, and reliability are asserted. Before we even consider the judgments of God, we see the ground, the basis, and the foundation for his judgments. He doesn't judge because he is wicked, delights in evil, or is somehow

7   For a brief discussion of the meaning of righteousness in Paul, with attention to the Old Testament background, see Thomas R. Schreiner, *Romans,* 2nd ed., BECNT (Grand Rapids, MI: Baker Academic, 2018), 66–78.

8   See the discussion in Brendan Byrne, *Romans,* Sacra Pagina (Collegeville, MN: Liturgical Press, 1996), 57–58, 65–66. Byrne, incidentally, agrees that God's righteousness can't be separated from judgment.

perversely sadistic. He judges because he is perfect in righteousness so that he is unstained and uncontaminated by evil.

David affirms, in a context where the wicked are trying to destroy him, that

> the LORD is righteous;
> he loves righteous deeds. (Ps. 11:7)

The order of the clauses here is important. First, we are told that the Lord *is righteous*; that is his character and nature, that is who he is ontologically. First comes being, then doing. Since the Lord is inherently and intrinsically righteous, he loves righteous actions. We fear authorities over us if they are twisted by evil or if they reward those who are corrupt, unethical, and immoral. But we respect and honor an authority who is righteous and who takes pleasure in what is good. The self-revelation of the Lord indicates that he is infinitely perfect—a God who is pure and unsullied goodness, who takes delight when human beings live righteously. It makes perfect sense, then, that God rewards those who practice goodness. The logic is again simple and clear: "The LORD is righteous; he loves righteous deeds" (Ps. 11:7; cf. Ps. 9:4).

If the Lord is righteous, loves righteousness, and rewards righteousness, then the converse follows as well. His love of righteousness also means that evil will be frowned on and punished. We see this several times in the Old Testament. When the southern kingdom of Judah under Rehoboam is disciplined for departing from the Lord, they confess that their punishment is deserved, declaring, "The LORD is righteous" (2 Chron. 12:6). Ezra confesses the sins of Israel in Ezra 9:1–15. He acknowledges that all the sorrow and pain Israel experienced was deserved, that God was righteous on account of the guilt of the nation (Ezra 9:15), while at the same time remembering the Lord's mercy to his people. Nehemiah, writing at the same time as Ezra (in the 400s, after Israel had been exiled and had then returned to the land), gives us a tour of Israel's history. He emphasizes the covenant unfaithfulness of the nation, their constant swerving from the Lord's ways. Thus he declares about the Lord, "Yet you have been righteous in all that has come upon us, for you have dealt faithfully and we have acted wickedly" (Neh. 9:33). The judgments Israel experienced substantiate Yahweh's rectitude.

We find the same sentiment earlier in Israel's history. Daniel prays that the promise of Jeremiah (Jer. 25:11–12; 29:10), which pledges that the nation would return to the land after seventy years, would be fulfilled. Like Ezra and Nehemiah, Daniel confesses the sins of Israel. When he comes to the exile he says, "The LORD has kept ready the calamity and has brought it upon us, for the LORD our God is righteous in all the works that he has done, and we have not obeyed his voice" (Dan. 9:14). The logic is exactly the same that we saw above. Since God is righteous, he loves and rewards good deeds. But it stands to reason as well that since God is righteous, he punishes evil.

Righteousness and goodness are compromised if evil is tolerated, ignored, and overlooked, especially when one has the power to resist wickedness. Even though judgment is often thought to be cruel, the opposite is the case. An authority who indulgently allows evil to occur without any consequence is not righteous but wicked. Thus, the psalmist praises Yahweh,

God is a righteous judge,
    and a God who feels indignation every day. (Ps. 7:11)

The cause-and-effect logic already noted stands out again. Since God is righteous, evil that is perpetrated must have a response, and God's response is a daily occurrence.

This is not to say, of course, that all evil is judged immediately, since God is also merciful, and the relation between justice and mercy must also be taken into account. The relationship between judgment and mercy is complex, and it can't be reduced to a formula, since mercy can't be calculated through a mathematical equation. It suffices to say that justice and wrath are not enemies but friends, not adversaries but allies. God's wrath is an expression and manifestation of his justice.

Nor is God's judgment superficial, since he tests "the minds and hearts" (Ps. 7:9). His judgments penetrate to the heart of the matter; they square with the intentions and motives that animate human beings since, as one who is infinitely wise and infinitely knowledgeable, he knows the thoughts and motives of all. As Proverbs 16:2 says,

> All the ways of a man are pure in his own eyes,
>   but the LORD weighs the spirit.

All of this is to say that the Lord's judgments are truly righteous. He doesn't judge from a partial perspective. He judges with infinite wisdom and knowledge as one who sees and knows all of reality, including the actions of human beings and the motives behind the actions.

God Is Just

Justice and righteousness overlap semantically, and this is evident since the word "justice" was used several times in the previous discussion. We should not drive a wedge between the terms. They are overlapping synonyms: justice means that God is fair, equitable, and good. Isaiah declares,

> The LORD of hosts is exalted in justice,
>   and the Holy God shows himself holy in righteousness. (Isa. 5:16)

As with holiness and righteousness, justice isn't a virtue to which God conforms. Instead, God *is* just; he is intrinsically and inherently righteous so that justice constitutes God's very being. Psalm 89:14 avers, "Righteousness and justice are the foundation of your throne."

Because God is just, we are not surprised to read that he loves justice (Ps. 33:5) and that he delights in justice (Jer. 9:24), which is really another way of saying that the Lord delights in himself since he enshrines perfection. The Lord doesn't need anyone to teach or instruct him about the nature of justice; rather, his very being is just (Isa. 40:14). As Isaiah 61:8 says,

I the LORD love justice;
    I hate robbery and wrong.

Loving justice means that the converse is also the case. God hates all injustice, referring to any situation where human beings are oppressed, mistreated, or abused. The Lord hates injustice because it is ugly, defacing, deforming, and devasting, contrary to the character of God himself.

Since God is just and righteous, his judgments are fair (Pss. 9:8; 67:4; 96:13; 98:9). Such statements may be easily passed over as we read them; they seem quite obvious to those who read Scripture. Still, these affirmations are fundamental and critical since they show that biblical writers were concerned about whether God's judgments were equitable and warranted. The Lord is just, so he will come to the aid of those in covenant with him who are beleaguered and mistreated.

With righteousness he shall judge the poor,
    and decide with equity for the meek of the earth. (Isa. 11:4)

The Lord's intervention for the poor and oppressed among his people is a common theme (Pss. 82:2–4; 103:6; 140:12; 146:7; Ezek. 34:20, 22).[9] The Lord judges according to a standard, according to what people do (Ezek. 7:3, 8; 18:30). In other words, his judgment is retributive so that people are recompensed according to their behavior, according to what they have done.[10] In his prayer when the temple was built, Solomon sums up God's standard of judgment: "Hear in heaven and act and judge your servants, condemning the guilty by bringing his conduct on his own head, and vindicating the righteous by rewarding him according to his righteousness" (1 Kings 8:32). God's justice means that everyone

9   The poor among God's people, of course, are also wicked in and of themselves and, therefore, deserve judgment. But in the texts noted above, the poor are those saved by the mercy of God who now live in ways that please God; thus, they are rewarded for their righteousness. Such a reward is just, but since their obedience is imperfect, the reward is also merciful.

10 On this theme, see also Morris, *The Biblical Doctrine of Judgment*, 47–48.

receives his or her due, everyone is assessed by the same standard. No one receives a raw deal.

Still, people questioned God's justice. The cynics of Malachi's day queried, "Where is the God of justice?" (Mal. 2:17). Job is reproved, even though he was mainly in the right in his debate with his friends, for questioning God's justice and exalting his own (Job 8:3; 34:12; 40:8). Habakkuk's prophecy opens a fascinating window on God's justice. The book begins with Habakkuk lamenting the violence, injustice, and lawlessness in the southern kingdom of Judah (Hab. 1:2–4). The Lord's failure to respond in judgment surprises and even scandalizes Habakkuk, from which we see incidentally that the Lord is patient, doesn't judge immediately, and gives people time to repent. Still, the Lord answers Habakkuk's query, affirming that he will judge Judah by means of the fierce and relentless Babylonian armies (Hab. 1:5–11). God's answer plunges Habakkuk into a deeper quandary, since the Babylonians were known for their godlessness and ferocity. The prophet questions God's justice since a nation that was more evil than Judah would be the agent of judgment (Hab. 1:12–17). The Lord answers this query in Habakkuk 2, assuring the prophet that the day of Babylon's judgment would also come. Habakkuk paints a complex picture of God's judgment so that we eschew simplistic formulas in our conception of justice. God's judgment isn't the only dimension of God's nature and character. He is also patient and merciful and, thus, doesn't judge immediately, reserving in his wisdom the time when judgment is right. Human beings cannot and do not see the whole picture; every facet of reality isn't disclosed to us, and thus we cannot assess when judgment should be levied. The timing of judgment, then, must be left to God, and human beings must not dictate to him when judgment should be carried out.

We think of the destruction of the Canaanites that occurred when Israel inherited the land under Joshua. Many questions about the occupation arise that can't be unpacked and discussed here. We do know the land of Canaan was promised to Abram much earlier, but the Lord informs Abram that the promise will not be realized for four generations since "the iniquity of the Amorites is not yet complete" (Gen.

15:16). We should note the timing of the judgment. Even in Abram's day, the Amorites were evil, and yet their evil had not yet reached the level that warranted expulsion and destruction. God explained to Abram that the day of reckoning was coming, a day when the expulsion, annihilation, and destruction of the Amorites would be just and righteous, a day when their sins deserved complete removal from the land. The account of the Canaanites and the words in Genesis 15:16 reveal that biblical writers were aware that such a judgment needed an explanation and that drastic measures were needed for drastic situations. At the end of the day, God is the Lord of life and death, determining the destiny of every person. Every question we ask isn't answered, but the fundamental question is whether we will trust in God's goodness and righteousness in his rule over the world.

God's righteous judgment as it is explained in Habakkuk may raise other questions, such as how God can use the Babylonians, who are even more wicked than Judah, to judge his people. The Lord doesn't rebuke Habakkuk for asking the question, revealing that questions are acceptable and natural. They are not rejected as unreasonable when raised with the right spirit and tone.[11] Still, the Lord's plan to enact justice may provoke objections and questions that can't be resolved immediately, especially when nations and people that are shockingly corrupt are the agents. Ultimately, every person and nation will be assessed fairly and proportionately, but much is hidden from us so that we typically don't perceive the equity of his judgment (or perhaps even the reality of it) during our earthly sojourn.

Such reflections bring us to one of the most famous judgments in the Bible and in history, where the Lord rained fire and brimstone down on Sodom, Gomorrah, and a couple of smaller cities (Gen. 19). The angel of the Lord informed Abraham about what was looming for Sodom and Gomorrah because of its wickedness (Gen. 18). Upon learning what

---

11   We see this dynamic in the questions raised by Zechariah and Mary in Luke's Gospel. See Thomas R. Schreiner, *Luke*, in *Matthew–Luke*, vol. 8 of *ESV Expository Commentary*, ed. Iain M. Duguid, James M. Hamilton Jr., and Jay Sklar (Wheaton, IL: Crossway, 2021), 731, 736.

was in store for Sodom, Abraham interceded, entreating the Lord to spare the city if there were fifty righteous people, then forty-five, then forty, then thirty, then twenty—all the way down to ten. Each time, the Lord assured Abraham that he would spare the city if the requisite number of righteous were reached. In Genesis 19, of course, the cities were obliterated, but several features of God's justice stand out as the prayer of Abraham is answered.

First, no one suffers the judgment who didn't deserve it. It becomes apparent that there was only one righteous person in the city—namely, Lot. There were not even the ten that Abraham hoped and prayed lived there. Still, the Lord answered Abraham's prayer in that he did not "sweep away the righteous with the wicked" (Gen. 18:23). He rescued the one righteous person in the city, and thus he went beyond what Abraham asked or thought (Eph. 3:20). We are comforted and assured that no one is judged unfairly. God spares any who turn away from evil. Also, the evil of Sodom and Gomorrah had accumulated for a long time. God is patient; he didn't judge immediately. Even in judgment, he also shows mercy. Even though Lot was the only righteous person in Sodom, he was spared from judgment since he was a righteous person (cf. 2 Pet. 2:7–9).[12]

Second, another way of putting it is reflected in Abraham's intercession. Abraham's intercession is amazingly bold and frank, sounding almost like a reproof of God when he says about the possible destruction of the cities, "Far be it from you to do such a thing, to put the righteous to death with the wicked, so that the righteous fare as the wicked! Far be that from you! Shall not the Judge of all the earth do what is just?" (Gen. 18:25). Abraham's words reveal an important truth about God's justice, one that seems elementary but that is also vital. God doesn't treat the righteous and the wicked in the same way. Judgment is meted out only and exclusively to the wicked. The reason for this is that God,

---

12   Scripture also teaches that no one is righteous, that all fall short, that all are sinners (Rom. 3:9–20, 23). What we see in Genesis and 2 Peter is that Lot has been changed (though not perfectly) by God's grace; his life, despite his shortcomings, is appropriately described as "righteous."

as the Judge of the whole earth, does what is just and right. No one anywhere will face final punishment who doesn't deserve it. We don't need to worry about whether some will be excluded from God's presence unfairly, for we will see on the final day that God's judgments are just. We will not object about the recompense assigned to any person. We will see more clearly than we do now the righteousness of God's judgments, and thus we are summoned to trust God's character and God's justice, as we consider his judgments in history and at the final judgment.

Third, God discloses to Abraham, as his covenant partner, his intention to destroy the cities of the plain. In doing so he invited Abraham to pray, to intercede, to ask God to spare those who are in the right. In the wisdom of God, human beings play a role and participate in what happens in history. We are not the final judge, and we are certainly not the Lord, but neither are we pieces on a chess board nor puppets in God's plan. We play a vital and mysterious role as the Lord works out his will and righteous judgments in the world. As New Testament believers, we proclaim the good news of salvation in Jesus Christ to those who are separated from God, inviting them to put their faith in Christ and to escape the judgment to come.

Fourth, the judgment of Sodom and Gomorrah was a temporal judgment, a judgment in history, but the New Testament picks up the story and applies what happened in history typologically to the final judgment (Matt. 10:15; 11:23–24; Luke 10:12; 17:29; 2 Pet. 2:6; Jude 7). We saw that New Testament writers picked up this same theme relative to the flood as well. Judgments in history point to and anticipate the final judgment. We must be careful, of course, since it isn't necessarily the case that all those who perish in temporal judgments will also be judged eternally. But the judgment of Sodom and Gomorrah is typologically escalated in the New Testament so that it becomes an adumbration of the judgment to come.

Fifth, perhaps the saddest words in the narrative about Sodom surface when Lot told his sons-in-law to flee the city since it was destined for destruction. They refused to heed his advice because they thought that what he said was amusing, that he was joking (Gen. 19:14). These words are poignant because they also reflect the stance of many in our culture today. We may see in a movie or TV show an angry preacher who seems to relish and enjoy telling people that they will go to hell if they don't repent. Many of our contemporaries respond to such a preacher with amusement and a sense of self-righteousness since the preacher's threats clearly reflect his own vindictiveness and joylessness. But such caricatures don't mean that there isn't a judgment—as many seem to think today. Satan has convinced many that any threat of judgment is merely a joke. In doing so, he has the last laugh, which is tragic indeed.

Conclusion

We see in the Old Testament that God's judgments are anchored in his holiness, his justice, and his righteousness. God's justice isn't vindictive, arbitrary, whimsical, or capricious. Nor does God strike out in judgment immediately. He longs to show mercy, inviting people to repent, giving them time to turn back to him. This is beautifully expressed by Ezekiel. "For I have no pleasure in the death of anyone, declares the Lord GOD; so turn, and live" (Ezek.18:32). Isaiah reminds us that judgment is the Lord's "strange work . . . his alien task" (Isa. 28:21 NIV). We should not misinterpret the latter statement. It is not as if judgment doesn't accord with who God is—his holiness and justice. The point is that the Lord doesn't delight in judgment in the same way that he delights in mercy, in grace, or in saving his people. We see the same truth in Lamentations 3:33: God "does not afflict from his heart or grieve the children of men." Certainly, there are mysteries about God's sovereign plans, purposes, and being that we can't attend to here.[13] In any case, the Lord's patience doesn't last forever. Evil can't be tolerated indefinitely. There comes a day when evil will be reckoned with—when it will be judged and when people

---

13   For instance, I think divine simplicity accords with the biblical witness, but that subject will not be examined here. For a helpful discussion of the simplicity of God, see, e.g., Scott R. Swain, *The Trinity: An Introduction*, SSST (Wheaton, IL: Crossway, 2020), 53–63.

will receive the consequences for what they deserve. We see this in the Old Testament as historical judgments are righteously meted out to those who gave themselves to evil. These judgments in history forecast the final judgment, the day to come, when all will stand before God.

2

The Ugliness of Sin

For all have sinned and fall short of the glory of God.

ROMANS 3:23

Introduction

Judgment doesn't take place in a vacuum; it is not arbitrary, whimsical, or capricious. As we saw in the previous chapter, judgment takes place for a reason, and the reason is human sin. Sin deserves judgment: it denies God's lordship, deforms human beings, wars against truth, and destroys human community. The Lord of hosts is beautiful and lovely in his holiness, and sin is ugly and defacing. We could say that sin denies the truth and denies reality—and God himself is truth and reality. Anything contrary to reality must be set right since what is false cannot be allowed to stand. God is holy, righteous, and just, and sin warrants judgment and the wrath of God because it is unholy, unrighteous, and unjust.

Various words are used in Scripture to describe this state of affairs, such as *sin, transgression,* and *iniquity.* The biblical writers also draw on cultic language so that those who sin are described as *unclean, impure, defiled, filthy, corrupt,* and *detestable.* In addition, sin is painted as *treachery,* as *unfaithfulness,* as *adultery*—all of which are ways of portraying idolatry. In this chapter, some snapshots of sin will be taken so that we get a sense for why sin warrants judgment.

Sin

The word "sin" (Hebrew *ht'* and Greek *hamartia* and *hamartanō*) has the idea of missing the mark (Job 5:24; Prov. 19:2). In Judges 20:16, those who sling stones are so skilled that they don't miss the mark; they "sin" (in a secular sense) if they *miss* their target. When the standard missed is one set by God, then sin is profoundly theological. For instance, Joseph refused to have a sexual dalliance with Potiphar's wife since doing so would constitute sin against God (Gen. 39:9). Joseph could have reflected only on the damage to Potiphar as the husband, but sin constitutes a refusal to live under God's lordship and brings him dishonor. Hophni and Phinehas as the sons of Eli, as priests, were in mortal danger since they didn't merely sin against human beings but also against God himself (1 Sam. 2:25). Of course, there is also the recognition that one can miss the mark by sinning against others so that Joseph's brothers sinned against him by selling him into slavery (Gen. 50:20).

In the Old Testament, sins violate the torah—the law given by God—particularly when one violates the Ten Commandments: by dishonoring parents (Prov. 28:24), by committing murder (Gen. 4:7–8), by engaging in adultery or other sexual sin (2 Sam. 12:13; 1 Cor. 6:18), by stealing (Gen. 31:36–37; Josh. 7:11), by worshiping other gods (Ex. 32:30–31; 1 Kings 13:33–34; Jer. 17:1–3), and so on. The commands themselves are important, and yet we should also realize that disobedience represents rebellion against Yahweh as covenant Lord, as the sovereign and redeemer of his people. Sin is also a universal reality (1 Kings 8:46; Prov. 20:9; Eccl. 7:20) so that no one is exempted from the charge of sin. The New Testament also affirms that sin is universal (Rom. 3:23; 1 John 1:8, 10) and that all are enslaved to sin (Rom. 6:6, 14, 16, 18, 20, 22) as sons and daughters of Adam (Rom. 5:12–19). Sin is a power, a force, that controls the lives of human beings; they live under its power and sway.

Transgression

Another common word for sin in the Old Testament is the Hebrew *pesha*ʿ, which is used in various ways. In some instances it seems to denote a crime (Gen. 31:36; Ex. 22:8; 1 Sam. 24:11; Amos 1:3, 6), while in others it may denote rebellious actions (Ex. 23:21; Lev. 16:16), and in still others transgressions (Josh. 24:19; Ezek. 33:10, 12), though the distinctions drawn in these various contexts should probably not be pressed.

In the New Testament, the Greek words *paraptōma* and *parabasis* usually mean "transgression" (Matt. 6:14, 15; Rom. 2:23; 4:25; 5:14, 15, 16; 2 Cor. 5:19; Eph. 1:7; 1 Tim. 2:14; Heb. 2:2; 9:15), though the terms can't always be distinguished clearly from the word "sin" (*hamartia*). When the term *pesha*ʿ means "transgression" in the Old Testament, it denotes a violation of what God commanded, a refusal to stay within the limits he has prescribed, a stepping over the line or the boundary that God has set. "Transgression" in the New Testament has to do with specifically revealed laws or stipulations that are flouted. Thus, Paul says that there is only transgression where there is law (Rom. 4:15). He doesn't mean by this that there isn't sin apart from the law, since in Romans 2:12 he declares that Gentiles who sin without having the law will perish apart from the law. Romans 2:12 teaches us something very important: people can sin even if there isn't a law forbidding a particular action. Romans 4:15 shines the light on another dimension of reality: one stands guilty of transgression in a technical sense where one violates a written or published law, command, or statute.

Along the same lines, those who died in the time between Adam and Moses were sinners (Rom. 5:13–14), and this is evident because they died, revealing that death is the punishment for sin (Rom. 6:23). Still, those who died in the time between Adam and Moses were not guilty of a transgression like Adam, since the latter violated God's specific command not to eat of the tree of the knowledge of good and evil (Rom. 5:14). All sin warrants punishment, but transgression has an edge, a provocative flavor: it flouts what God has specifically forbidden. When God gives commands, he clarifies what is right and good, removing any ambiguity or question about the right course of action. When we as human beings fail to keep these precepts, sin's audacity and outrageousness are displayed. We proclaim to God and to the world that we are the standard of right and wrong, that no one can tell us what to do, that we are our own masters and commanders, and that we are the ultimate arbiters of right and wrong. Violating revealed laws connotes rebellion, since those who disobey a written command spurn the authority of the one who gives the command. Paul reflects in Romans 7:7–12 on the role that commands play in the lives of the unregenerate, explaining how the command itself may precipitate the desire to violate it, uncovering the mutinous spirit in the human heart.

Iniquity

The term "iniquity" (*'awon*) is quite interesting. Etymology can lead us astray in understanding a word, but in some cases, it can prove illuminating. In the case of the Hebrew word, the etymology aids in understanding.[1] We see a verbal form in Psalm 38:6, in the phrase, "I am utterly bowed down," and in Isaiah 24:1, where we are told that that the Lord "will twist" the "surface" of the earth. We see that the word can be defined "to bend, curve, turn aside, twist."[2] The term "iniquity," then, is another way of describing sin or transgression, and this is evident in many texts (Deut. 19:15; 2 Sam. 7:14; 24:17; 1 Kings 8:47; Pss. 103:3; 106:6; Isa. 64:6; Jer. 3:21; Lam. 2:14; Dan. 9:5; Amos 3:2; Mic. 7:19). What is particularly interesting as we consider the etymology of the word is that the term "iniquity" signals that sin twists, distorts, deforms, and warps human beings. Sin, in a sense, makes us less human since it puts us out of joint so that we don't function as intended.

Another interesting dimension of this term is that it often occurs in contexts where it points to the guilt we bear because of sin. Thus, in Genesis 4:13, Cain says, "My punishment [*'awoni*] is greater than I can

---

1   In the LXX, various words are used to translate the Hebrew term, including "sin" (*hamartia, hamartēma*), "lawlessness" (*anomia*), and "unrighteousness" (*adikia*).
2   Rolf Knierim, "עָוֹן," in *TLOT* 2.863.

bear." In this instance, both the sin and the consequence of sin are in view. So too, in 2 Kings 7:9, the lepers who fortuitously discovered the riches that the Syrians left in haste realized that their iniquity in not telling others about their discovery would lead to punishment if they didn't share the good news. The close connection between iniquity and guilt surfaces in Psalm 25:11,

> For your name's sake, O LORD,
>   pardon my guilt, for it is great.

Similarly, we read in Psalm 31:10,

> My strength fails because of my iniquity,
>   and my bones waste away.

What is of interest is the bond forged between sin and punishment so that the term "iniquity" in some contexts denotes both the sin and the outcome, result, or consequence (guilt) of the sin. It is recognized that there is an inherent and intrinsic penalty to sin so that sin has a self-imploding dimension. Sin warrants negative consequences; it inevitably saddles one with guilt so that one who sins deserves to be punished.

Now, one could explain this in terms of cause and effect, and certainly sin has a cause-and-effect dimension in that God structured the world so that actions have consequences. Still, we must avoid a mechanistic conception of what happens—as if the biblical writers operate from within a deistic worldview. God does not set a process in motion that is disconnected from his person and will. In the scriptural frame of reference, rain, snow, frost, hail, and wind all come from God himself (Ps. 147:8–18). Furthermore, disasters aren't merely cause-and-effect realities. Amos 3:6 says,

> Does disaster come to a city,
>   unless the LORD has done it?

This verse means that the Lord has ordained that both the disaster and judgment would take place. Or as Lamentations 3:38 declares,

> Is it not from the mouth of the Most High
>   that good and bad come?

Many other texts could be adduced to substantiate the notion that God rules providentially over the world so that his purposes are realized (e.g., Isa. 46:9–11; Eph. 1:11).

The matter is too large to examine here, but the purpose for bringing it up is to certify that the punishment that comes from iniquity stems from God himself. God set up the universe to function as he willed, and he isn't absent from the world he created. He is always and ever the personal God, recompensing both the righteous and wicked according to what is right. We see here an example of retributive justice in that punishment and iniquity are bound together in a package.[3] The punishment following from iniquity is warranted since there is deed-consequence reality.

Filthiness

Sin is also defined as uncleanness, defilement, and impurity. Uncleanness is associated with ritual and ceremonial matters often in the Old Testament (e.g., Lev. 11:25, 26; 12:2, 5; 13:11, 25; 15:2, 3; 17:15), though sacrifices are offered to remove uncleanness, which could suggest that ritual uncleanness is sin. Most scholars agree, however, that ceremonial uncleanness doesn't signify personal sin even if sacrifices are offered for purification. On the other hand, ceremonial uncleanness communicates that there is something wrong with the world, that there is impurity and filth that needs to be removed. In that sense, ritual impurity signals and points to a deeper reality. We are not surprised, then, to find that the language of uncleanness is also applied to personal sins. Thus, the

---

3   For the notion of retributive judgment in the Old Testament, see John R. Coulson, *The Righteous Judgment of God: Aspects of Judgment in Paul's Letters* (Eugene, OR: Wipf & Stock, 2016), 3.

high priest on the Day of Atonement offers an atoning sacrifice for the Holy Place that is defiled because of Israel's impurity (Lev. 16:16). Isaiah declares, "I am a man of unclean lips, and I dwell in the midst of a people of unclean lips" (Isa. 6:5). He also confesses,

> We have all become like one who is unclean,
>   and all our righteous deeds are like a polluted garment.
>   (Isa. 64:6)

Israel was sent into exile because it was unclean (Lam. 1:9; Ezek. 22:15; 24:11; 36:17, 29; 39:24). Similarly, the Pharisees appeared to be pure on the outside, but on the inside they were full of uncleanness (Matt. 23:27–28). Paul uses the term "uncleanness" to designate sexual impurity (Rom. 1:24; 2 Cor. 12:21; Gal. 5:19; Eph. 5:3; Col. 3:5; 1 Thess. 4:7) and perhaps more generally to describe sin (Eph. 4:19; 1 Thess. 2:3). Believers are also summoned to abstain from all uncleanness (2 Cor. 6:17), since such a lifestyle doesn't accord with the new creation that has dawned (2 Cor. 5:17).

Sexual sin is also described using the verb "defile" (Hebrew *tm'* and Greek *miainō*) on a number of occasions (Gen. 34:5, 13, 27; 49:4; Num. 5:13, 14, 19, 20, 27, 28, 29; Deut. 24:4; Jer. 3:1, 2; Ezek. 18:11, 15; 22:11; 23:7, 13, 17; Hos. 5:3; 6:10; Jude 8), though defilement may be ritual or ceremonial as well (Lev. 5:3; 11:24, 43; 13:3). Jesus explains that foods don't "defile" (*koinoō*) a person (Mark 7:18). Defilement comes from within (Mark 7:23). "For from within, out of the heart of man, come evil thoughts, sexual immorality, theft, murder, adultery, coveting, wickedness, deceit, sensuality, envy, slander, pride, foolishness" (Mark 7:21–22). Ritual and ceremonial defilement aren't where the real problem lies. Something is profoundly wrong with us; we are stained, unclean, and filthy within. Such moral impurity manifests itself, as Jesus indicates, in countless ways.

The idolatrous practices of those living in Canaan, before the days when Israel inherited the land under Joshua, are described as defiling (Lev. 18:24, 25, 27, 28, 30); and sexual sin, given the content of the chapter as a whole, is probably particularly in view. Similarly, those who offer their children to Molech defile God's sanctuary (Lev. 20:3), and those who practice idolatry (Ezek. 5:11; 7:22; 20:7, 18, 30, 31; 22:3, 4; 37:23) profane God's sanctuary and themselves as well. The Holy One of Israel can't dwell with a people who have given themselves to uncleanness. The word "defilement" also captures the behavior of Israel and Judah before they were thrust into exile (Ps. 106:39; Jer. 2:7, 23; 7:30; Ezek. 14:11; 20:43; 36:17; cf. Hag. 2:14), explaining why they were expelled from the land. We see again that sin exacts retributive punishment, that fitting consequences follow the commission of sin.

Since sin stains and defiles, it follows that sin is ugly and filthy. It takes what is beautiful and sullies and tarnishes it. Sin doesn't ennoble human beings but casts us into the mire so that we are disfigured and scarred. Sin can be likened to throwing dirt on a beautiful painting of Van Gogh or spewing the muck of the sewer on Michelangelo's sculpture of David. We all judge and condemn what is filthy and dirty, whether it is litter in a lovely park or graffiti defacing a beautiful mural. So, too, God judges sin for what it is. That which is defiled and tainted can't remain in his presence, since only what is beautiful and lovely remains. An analogy to God's judgment of sin (and it is only an analogy!) exists when we clean up what is defiled and dirty. We remove litter from a city park because it defaces and scars a park. Typically wedding dresses are beautifully white in that they symbolize the purity and goodness of getting married, and no one would tolerate a wedding dress spattered intentionally with mud. God is indescribably lovely and pure, and because of his goodness, only what is pure, only what is clean, only what is undefiled can have fellowship with him.

Corruption

Using a metaphor that is somewhat similar to uncleanness, Scripture also describes sin as "corruption" (Hebrew *shahat* and Greek *phtheirō*, *phthora*). God judged the earth with a flood because it was "corrupt" (Gen. 6:11, 12). Moses predicted after his death that Israel would become radically and completely corrupt (Deut. 31:29). All people everywhere without exception are indicted for their corruption, for their failure to do what is good and right and true (Pss. 14:1; 53:1; Rom. 3:12);[4] and the covenant people, Israel, demonstrated their corruption, sometimes in remarkably perverted ways (Judg. 2:19; Jer. 6:28; Ezek. 16:47; 20:44; Zeph. 3:7). The corruption in the world stems from evil desires (Eph. 4:22; 2 Pet. 1:4), showing that selfish lusts drive human behavior. It is not surprising, then, that human beings may become "slaves of corruption" (2 Pet. 2:19).

The corruption of sin is self-destructive,

> He who commits adultery lacks sense;
>> he who does it destroys himself. (Prov. 6:32)

Paul claims in his ministry that he has "corrupted no one" (2 Cor. 7:2), standing in contrast with Babylon, which has "corrupted the earth" (Rev. 19:2). In the Old Testament, the word "corruption" represents that which is marred, such as the appearance of the servant of the Lord (Isa. 52:14). It can stand for what is ruined, such as Egypt blighted by flies (Ex. 8:24) or the underwear Jeremiah hid near the Euphrates (Jer. 13:7). Similarly, it can refer to what is destroyed, such as the potter destroying what he made from the clay (Jer. 18:4), the destruction of an eye (Ex. 21:26), the killing of a human being (2 Sam. 14:11), or people being destroyed or killed in battle (Judg. 20:21; 2 Sam. 11:1).

In the New Testament the term refers to the destruction of a temple (1 Cor. 3:17) and to the corruption and ruin coming at the final judgment (2 Pet. 2:12). Corruption paints sin as something that ruins and blights and unravels our lives. Paul says that the "old self . . . is corrupt through deceitful desires" (Eph. 4:22). The desires deceive because they promise we will achieve wholeness and life if we pursue them, but in fact these desires lead to our undoing. We end up becoming a shadow

---

4 The Greek word here is *achreioō*.

of what we were intended to be. We see this with a person who wastes away because of alcohol or drug addiction, or a person who has a critical spirit so that they spend their time maligning and running down others. In judging the corrupt, God acts against what isn't beautiful, removing from his presence what leads to death and destruction.

Detestable and Depraved

The Bible labels sin as "abominable" or "detestable" (Hebrew *to'evah* and Greek *bdelygma*), and sometimes the description is rather general so that precise sins aren't mentioned (Ezek. 5:9, 11; 7:3, 4, 8, 9; 11:18; 36:31; cf. Ezra 9:1, 11, 14). Nevertheless, some specific examples are given. For instance, burning sons and daughters as an offering to other gods is a monstrous crime (Deut. 12:31; 18:9–10; 2 Kings 16:3; 2 Chron. 28:3; Jer. 32:35), but so are corrupt and evil financial transactions (Deut. 25:13–16; Prov. 20:10, 23) and murder (Ezek. 22:2–4). Judges who don't adjudicate rightly and justly also do what is detestable (Prov. 17:15). Sexual relations with someone of the same sex or with an animal is abhorrent (Lev. 18:22, 23; 20:13; cf. Deut. 23:18 [23:19 MT]; 1 Kings 14:24), as is wearing clothing of the opposite sex (Deut. 22:5). All the sexual sins in Leviticus 18 are identified as monstrous abominations (Lev. 18:29, 30; see also Ezek. 22:10–11).

Similarly, idolatry is "detestable," as is consulting mediums or spiritists or practicing sorcery of any kind (Deut. 7:25, 26; 13:14 [13:15 MT]; 17:4; 18:10–12; 20:18; 27:15; 32:16; 2 Kings 23:13; Isa. 41:24; 44:19; Jer. 7:10; 16:18; Ezek. 6:9; 7:20; 8:6, 9; 16:22, 36; Mal. 2:11; Rev. 17:4, 5). Sacrificing an animal with defects and eating forbidden foods are also abominable (Deut. 14:3; 17:1), and so is worship without a right heart before the Lord (Prov. 15:8; 21:27; 28:9; Isa. 1:13).

Proverbs itemizes seven things that are detestable to the Lord:

> haughty eyes, a lying tongue,
>> and hands that shed innocent blood,
> a heart that devises wicked plans,
>> feet that make haste to run to evil,

a false witness who breathes out lies,
  and one who sows discord among brothers. (Prov. 6:17–19; cf.
    Prov. 8:7)

Indeed, pride is identified as abominable (Prov. 16:5), as is the claim of sinners that they are justified before God (Luke 16:15). Those who do what is abominable will be excluded from the book of life (Rev. 21:27).

A word that is in the same semantic range as detestable is "depravity" (Hebrew *zimmah*). Those who are morally foolish enjoy their decadence and degeneracy (Prov. 10:23). Depravity is present when one has sexual relations with a close relative (Lev. 18:17; 20:14; Ezek. 22:11). Similarly, prostitution and adultery are rejected as depraved (Lev. 19:29; Ezek. 22:11; Job 31:9–11). The rape, abuse, and murder of the concubine by the Benjaminites is one of the most infamous accounts of depravity in Israelite history (Judg. 20:6). The idolatry of Israel is also described (see more below) as sexual depravity (Jer. 13:27; Ezek. 16:27, 43, 58; 23:21, 27, 29, 35, 44, 48, 49), and murder is put in the same category as well (Hos. 6:9).

Another term that falls within the same scope as depravity and detestable is "foolishness" (Hebrew *nebalah* and Greek *aphrosynē*). The word "foolishness" doesn't describe one's intellectual capacities but one's moral stance in the world. Adultery is characterized as foolish (Deut. 22:21), as are the outrageous rape and murder carried out by the Benjaminites (Judg. 19:23, 24), the character of Nabal (1 Sam. 25:25), the rape of Tamar by Amnon (2 Sam. 13:12), and the consequences of giving way to a forbidden woman's sexual advances (Prov. 5:5, 23 LXX).

The sins described with words like "abominable," "detestable," "corruption," "depravity," and "foolishness" are outrageous and shocking. The biblical authors want us to see and to *feel* the degradation of sin so that we as readers are appalled and disgusted about sin and its effects. When we read stories of abuse, rape, sexual depravity, and murder, we cry out for justice, for someone somewhere to recompense the evils perpetrated in the world. We recognize in these accounts that there is something deeply wrong, that there is a cancer in human beings that leads to great evils. In the biblical worldview, God as the Judge (Ps. 50) will right all wrongs and see that justice is done. Evil will not finally triumph, and it will not be ignored or quietly forgotten. Those who continue in evil and who fail to repent will face the consequences of their decisions.

Rebellion and Adultery

Sin is also referred to in terms of "rebellion" (Hebrew *meri*; see Num. 17:10 [17:25 MT]; Deut. 31:27; Ezek. 2:8; 12:2; 17:12; 44:6). Remarkably, rebellion is put into the same category as divination (1 Sam. 15:23), showing that rebellion is akin to idolatry; and it falls under that category because rebellion indicates that self is god, that the highest court of appeal isn't God's will and ways but our own desires. Rebellion insists on doing things our way. Israel's stubbornness (Ex. 32:9; 33:3, 5; Deut. 9:13, 10:16; 31:27; 2 Kings 17:14; 2 Chron. 36:13; Neh. 9:16, 17; Prov. 29:1; Jer. 7:26; 17:23; Acts 7:51), which is captured nicely with the frequent expression "stiff-necked," also describes human wayward-ness. Stubbornness is intractable, immoveable, and obstinate, and the insistence on doing what we want to do is its root.

Other descriptions of sin could be included, but one of the most significant should be mentioned. The Old Testament often describes Israel's sin in terms of being a harlot or an adulterer. Israel is compared to a bride married to Yahweh, a bride who loved her husband during her youth (Jer. 2:2). She turned from such devoted love to prostitution, to worship of false gods (Jer. 2:20, 23–25, 32–35; 3:1–3). The descriptions of the faithlessness of Israel and Judah in Ezekiel 16 and 23 are shocking and scandalous, and thus they are rarely read in church (Ezek. 16:15–38, 43; 23:3–21, 29–30, 35, 37; 40–45, 48–49). The lurid language is designed to shock readers so that we will feel how reprehensible and outrageous it is to worship other gods. The people of God are as eager to commit idolatry as a prostitute, who longs to have sex with multiple partners. God opens a window on how he views our worship of anything other than himself, revealing to us the depth of our unfaithfulness. The prophecy of Hosea also describes Israel as a prostitute, as a nation eager to give sexual favors to those who come to her (Hos. 1:2; 2:2–5, 10, 13; 3:1–4). Once again, sexual imagery is deployed to illustrate Israel's idolatry. The New Testament picks up this theme in Revelation 17–18, where the city of Babylon—first-century imperial Rome—is described as a harlot, influencing the nations to drink the wine of her prostitution. Babylon's unfaithfulness leads her to slay the saints, to persecute the people of God.

Conclusion

We have seen in this chapter that sin misses the mark, that it can be described as transgression, rebellion, iniquity, and lawlessness, that it defiles and stains us so that it is detestable. Sin isn't merely a violation of the law, though it includes that as well. Sin is also treachery. It is compared to a wife who turns away from the kindest and most gracious husband imaginable, a husband who provided for her every need and rescued her from every danger, who loved her with sacrificial and tender love. Sin really doesn't make sense; it is a kind of insanity—a form of self-destruction where we turn against what fulfills and satisfies us, where we turn away from "the fountain of living waters" and dig "cisterns" for ourselves, "broken cisterns that can hold no water" (Jer. 2:13). Such actions aren't in our self-interest, and yet sin distorts the way we think and behave. Sin doesn't merely consist of wrong actions. When we sin, we abandon the Lord, we forsake *him*, and we refuse to love the one who has loved us. As Paul says in Romans 1:21, the fundamental sin is the failure to give thanks and praise to God, to acknowledge his goodness to us.

The serpent in the garden led Eve and Adam into sin by questioning God's goodness (Gen. 3:1–6), declaring that the tree of the knowledge of good and evil was withheld from the man and woman to limit their potential and power. The serpent claimed that God didn't really love them, that he was jealous for his own glory at the expense of their own flourishing, that he was afraid they would exalt themselves and become competitors. Thus, Adam and Eve also abandoned the Lord, holding him in suspicion, doubting his love and kind intentions toward them. At the end of the day, sin views God as satanic, as a malevolent being trying to destroy human lives. We come back to the notion that sin overturns the truth, that it doesn't accord with reality. Sin turns the world upside down by claiming that we are gods and that the true God doesn't deserve worship and praise. It sees the one true God as a demonic figure who only cares about himself but not about human beings. Such sin deserves judgment, for it can't be left unaddressed. Otherwise, God's goodness and holiness would be compromised.

Judgment in the Gospels and Acts

And these will go away into eternal punishment,
but the righteous into eternal life.

MATTHEW 25:46

Introduction

When we consider judgment in the Gospels and in the book of Acts, we find that Matthew refers to the judgment most often and Mark the least. The reason for this difference isn't hard to discover. Mark is an action-packed Gospel with few speeches, while Matthew's Gospel contains long discourses by Jesus. Almost all the references to the judgment appear in Matthew's discourses, most of which are lacking in Mark. John also stands out, not as contradicting the first three Gospels but by referring to the judgment in a characteristically Johannine way.

Despite the differences between the various writings, we see the pervasiveness of judgment. The coming judgment looms over all the Gospels and Acts, reminding readers that a day is approaching when the lives of all will be assessed and when the behavior of all will be recompensed. Instead of looking at each Gospel in turn, various texts on judgment will be clustered together for thematic reasons. The one exception is the Gospel of John. Given its distinctiveness, we will examine John separately.

In the study of the Synoptic Gospels and Acts, judgment will be considered under three themes: (1) verdict, (2) eternal destruction, and (3) anguish. These categories overlap, so some verses will be considered under more than one category, and not all verses neatly fit these three classifications. The three themes are a convenient way of considering the judgment but should not be understood as watertight compartments.

Verdict

Verdicts are declarations, decisions uttered and enforced by (in our case) the divine Judge. The word "judgment" often refers to a verdict of condemnation, and God's verdicts are always effective—they not only declare judgment but also effect it. We are in the orbit of verdicts as well in the following instances: when final woes are pronounced, when sins are measured, when God doesn't forgive people, when the Son of Man denies a person at the judgment, when a person isn't known by God at the final assize, and when one is sent away from God forever or toppled from his or her exalted place on earth.

I begin with forgiveness. Jesus declares that those who forgive others will be forgiven by God, but conversely those who don't forgive others will not receive divine forgiveness (Matt. 6:14–15). It isn't so much that God refuses to forgive some but that some refuse his forgiveness, choosing evil rather than repentance. Forgiveness has a legal dimension, and we see this in cases where debts are forgiven (Matt. 18:27). This theme is played out in the parable of the wicked servant who was forgiven by his master of an incalculable debt (Matt. 18:21–35). Still, this servant turned around and mercilessly and harshly refused to forgive the tiny debt another person owed him. Jesus warns us that those who refuse to forgive others, those who hold a grudge, those who insist that they can never forgive will be tortured and will never receive forgiveness from God (Matt. 18:34–35). Those who recognize that they have received divine mercy show mercy to others. If we don't forgive others, it reveals that we have never received the forgiveness that comes from God himself. It is evident from Matthew 6:14–15 and 18:21–35 that the forgiveness obtained or forfeited relates to life in the age to come and speaks to the future destiny of human beings. The texts also reveal that mercy is available, that judgment isn't inevitable, and that forgiveness may be obtained. All of this suggests that the verdict upon the unrepentant of *not forgiven* is deserved, since those offered mercy fail to show the same to others. Those who close their heart to others, those who withhold grace and mercy to those who have offended them, deserve to suffer the same fate from the divine Judge.

Jesus declares, in a famous saying, that those who blaspheme against the Holy Spirit won't be forgiven (Matt. 12:32; Mark 3:29; Luke 12:10), with Matthew adding, "either in this age or in the age to come," and Mark saying that they will "never" experience forgiveness because they are "guilty of an eternal sin." We don't need to expound here in detail on the nature of the blasphemy against the Spirit, though in the Matthean and Markan contexts it seems to center on attributing to the devil what is actually the work of the Holy Spirit. In Luke, the blasphemy follows the declaration that those who deny Jesus before human beings will be denied by Jesus before the angels (Luke 12:9). Forgiveness still avails for those who speak against the Son of Man (God is merciful!), but those who declaim against the Spirit won't receive forgiveness, and this isn't surprising since they look at divine works and attribute them to demonic powers. They contemplate perfect goodness and say that it is horribly evil. It should also be observed that the refusal to forgive those guilty of such blasphemy isn't limited to this age but also includes the one to come, showing that their failure to receive forgiveness has eternal consequences.

The negative verdict for human beings is often conveyed by the verb "judge" (*krinō*) or the nouns for "judgment" (*krima, krisis*) or by the noun "Judge" (*kritēs*) when speaking of God. Jesus was appointed by God as "judge of the living and the dead" (Acts 10:42), as the one who will pronounce on the fate of human beings on the last day. Paul in Athens declares that God "will judge the world in righteousness by a man whom he has appointed" (Acts 17:31), Jesus the Christ, adducing as proof that Jesus is risen from the dead. The addition of the words "in righteousness" are important, indicating that the judgment will accord with justice, that the judgment will set everything right so that the wrongs committed in this world will finally be redressed. "Both the just and the unjust" will be raised from the dead (Acts 24:15), and the Lord will righteously judge all on the last day.

Paul proclaims judgment to the Roman procurator Felix and his wife Drusilla, emphasizing "self-control" and "righteousness" (Acts 24:25). The talk of judgment frightened Felix so much that he sent Paul away because he wanted to put out of his mind such a future prospect. Felix's response mirrors many today who avoid entirely the notion that there will be a judgment, claiming that all will be saved, that no one will receive a negative verdict. We understand the sentiment behind such notions, but they are a denial of reality and contravene the biblical witness, which declares that a day of judgment is coming in which some will receive a negative verdict. The judgment has been delayed (Acts 14:16), and in the meantime God summons all to repent and to ready themselves for the impending day. Believers have a responsibility to tell others that a day of judgment is coming, and such a proclamation doesn't stem from anger or vindictiveness but from a heart of love, since we hope that all who hear the good news will repent and be saved from the final judgment.

Jewish law taught that one who murders is subject to judgment in human courts (Matt. 5:21), but Jesus goes further, saying that those who are angry and insult others will face an even more severe judgment in the divine hall of justice. The judgment in God's courts is irrevocable and horrible, for the destiny of the wicked is hell (Matt. 5:22). Jesus uses the illustration of being handed over to the judge and being thrown into prison, declaring that one will not be freed until the last cent has been paid (Matt. 5:25–26). The illustration should not be misinterpreted as if people will eventually pay the required sum and thus escape. Jesus speaks hyperbolically, and the point is that they will never get out of prison since they have no resources to pay the settlement.[1]

1   The Lukan version of this account should be interpreted similarly (Luke 12:58–59).

Judgment is also coming for those with unresolved or unrepentant anger—anger that isn't acknowledged or admitted. Amends can be made for such anger during this life as Jesus impresses upon his hearers the need to be reconciled to brothers or sisters if they have been harmed by our unrighteous anger. The refusal to apologize to others shows a hard heart before God, revealing a cold and sclerotic stance toward God himself.

What Jesus says about murder and anger discloses that sin isn't trivial in God's sight, that judgment is warranted not only for murder but also for anger directed toward others, for outbursts of anger that we don't turn from or apologize for. We could overinterpret this story in perfectionistic ways. What God looks at is our heart, the person we really are, whether we are humble and soft and flexible or whether we are self-righteous and angry and vindictive. We can both overinterpret and underinterpret what Jesus teaches here. We should readily acknowledge Luther's truth that we are *simul iustus et peccator*—"justified and at the same time sinners." Nevertheless, believers are new persons, and that newness should be manifested by our lives.

God's assessment of our lives reveals the inner depths of the human person so that human beings on the final day "will give account for every careless word they speak, for by your words you will be justified, and by your words you will be condemned" (Matt. 12:36–37). Morris, speaking of this text, says, "The thought that all we do matters in God's sight makes life worth living. It gives a dignity to even the most insignificant action, the most unimportant word."[2] It might seem that such a standard is irrational and could even be rejected as picayune. A closer look at the context, however, proves to be illuminating.

Jesus speaks of two different kinds of trees, both good and evil (Matt. 12:33–35). Good trees yield healthy fruit, while rotten trees produce spoiled and diseased fruit. The words that flow from our mouths disclose the inner person, and thus goodness will be evident from the words that emanate from our mouths. We see again that God judges

2   Leon Morris, *The Biblical Doctrine of Judgment* (Grand Rapids, MI: Eerdmans, 1960), 64.

the whole person, who we truly are, or perhaps we could also say, who we are truly becoming. Along the same lines, rotten words indicate that we are a "brood of vipers" (Matt. 12:34) so that there is a demonic and satanic character animating what is said. Judgment according to the words spoken isn't as trifling as it first appears, since the words spoken accord with who a person truly is, unveiling our character. Certainly the standard isn't perfection, since disciples are to pray regularly for forgiveness of sins (Matt. 6:12). The words that lead to condemnation flow from a heart opposed to Jesus Christ and the one true God.

Indeed, the context in Matthew 12 should be considered further because the Pharisees declared that Jesus expelled demons by Beelzebul instead of by the Spirit of God (Matt. 12:22–32). The Pharisees' own words condemned them, showing that they were the offspring of the serpent. They were so twisted that they called good evil, and this was not a minor misjudgment—they blasphemed the Spirit with their words by claiming that Jesus was demonic. The words they spoke represent the root sin because they declared that goodness in all its beauty and loveliness was actually satanic. Their words about Jesus indicated that they were not good trees, and thus judgment according to words isn't superficial but accords with what human beings truly are. Such judgment is according to truth.

Some have said that the most popular verse in the Bible is Jesus's command not to judge. Jesus warned against judging since it will lead to our own judgment and condemnation (Matt. 7:1; Luke 6:37). Now, this should not be interpreted to mean that all evaluation of the lives of others is forbidden. Even in the context of Jesus's command not to judge in Matthew's Gospel, his followers are commanded to be discerning so as not to throw what is holy to dogs (Matt. 7:6). Elsewhere, believers are enjoined to judge one another and to remove from the church those who are blatantly disobedient and unrepentant (1 Cor. 5:12–13). Such cases call for gentleness and the recognition that we are liable to fall into the same sins (Gal. 6:1) so that there is no room for being supercilious and superior. Having said all this, God has the prerogative to judge—something we as human beings don't possess.

As the Creator, as the sovereign Lord and King, he evaluates and assesses our lives (cf. James 4:11–12). Thus, judging others isn't so much wrong as it is blind: we fail to see that we indict ourselves by our very words of judgment. Our critical evaluation of others should, instead, cast us upon the mercy of God and lead us to be more merciful in our interactions with others because the day when we will be judged by the Creator of the universe is coming.

Jesus declared on more than one occasion that cities in Israel will face a severer judgment than Tyre, Sidon, Sodom, and Gomorrah (Matt. 10:15; 11:22–24; Luke 10:12–15). We see something similar in the claim that the people of Nineveh and the Queen of Sheba will condemn Jesus's generation since they responded to the divine message they heard in their day, while Jesus's contemporaries didn't respond to his overtures (Matt. 12:41–42; Luke 11:31–32). It seems that there are levels of judgment. Those who have received more revelation, those who have seen more clearly who Jesus truly is, are assessed more strictly. Luke 12:47–48 fits here because servants who know the will of their master will be punished more severely than those who did not perceive his will as clearly.[3] Both kinds of servants know the content of God's will, even if some see it with less clarity than others. Jesus declares that those who perceive the facts of the case, those who see reality clearly, recognize that judgment is warranted. In the person of Jesus, goodness and loveliness and perfection have entered the world, and yet many of the people in covenant with God—many in Israel—turned away from him. They didn't want to hear any message calling on them to change their lives. They desired affirmation, not correction; acceptance, not challenge; approval, not conviction. The judgment, then, in one sense represents their own choice in that they refused the revelation of God in Jesus. On the other hand, such a refusal

---

3   Stephen H. Travis, *Christ and the Judgement of God: The Limits of Divine Retribution in New Testament Thought* (Peabody, MA: Hendrickson, 2009), 239–40, admits that the text is difficult but is reluctant to see degrees of punishment, concluding that the text is about the extent of responsibility instead of the extent of punishment. The problem with this analysis is that the two notions are closely linked in the text and we don't have a basis for accepting the former and excluding the latter.

can't be tolerated forever since it would mean that lies are tolerated, that the truth of Jesus's person isn't upheld, that what is unrighteous is allowed to persist. Thus, God judges on the final day those who resist the truth about Jesus.

Some texts refer to Jesus not knowing a person relative to the final judgment. For example, Jesus will not know or acknowledge on the last day the five foolish virgins who didn't prepare their lamps by stocking them with oil (Matt. 25:12). Similarly, people are urged "to enter through the narrow door" before the Lord returns because some will be surprised when Jesus declares that he doesn't know them, and they will be excluded because of the evil that characterized their lives (Luke 13:22–27). Some who cast out demons, prophesy in Jesus's name, and perform mighty works will not receive approbation from the Lord on the last day (Matt. 7:21–23). He will declare that he "never knew" them since they lived lawlessly. God doesn't judge people based on their gifts but on the righteousness of their lives. There is a connection with Luke 6:44, since trees are "known" by the fruit they produce. Again, judgment coheres with reality, with the way things really are, with the true character and being of a person. The judgment isn't unfair or vindictive but recognizes human beings for what they truly are or, perhaps better, what they have truly become.

Another picture of this truth emerges in the parable of the barren fig tree (Luke 13:6–9). The vineyard owner expects fruit from the fig tree but finds it barren. He concludes that the tree is a lost cause since he has been seeking fruit from it for three years. Still, the laborer persuades the owner to give it more time and wait another year. Then if the tree doesn't yield figs, it should be cut down. The judgment is objective and retributive, based on whether the tree bears fruit. At the same time, the parable also reveals God's patience. He doesn't judge precipitously or immediately but gives people time to repent. God is merciful, looking for hearts that are soft and pliable, producing "deeds in keeping with their repentance" (Acts 26:20). Judgment is according to the truth, but the destiny of human beings isn't fixed. The Lord is generous, giving us time to repent, to turn away from evil, and to receive forgiveness—but the opportunity doesn't last forever. A day comes when trees are cut down if they haven't turned toward goodness.

Another fascinating parable is the story of the rich fool (Luke 12:16–21). The man isn't foolish because he is rich, since riches may represent God's blessing, nor is he foolish for saving and investing, since investing funds may be a means by which one helps others. The rich fool's horizon, however, is only his own future happiness, and he cares nothing for the needs of those around him. He has amassed riches and invested so that he can enjoy his retirement for years to come as he eats, drinks, and enjoys life. He has forgotten that he lives before God; the Lord may summon him into his presence at any time and demand an accounting. The word in Luke 12:20 for "demand" or "require" (*apaiteō*) often has a financial sense, where there is an accounting, a reckoning.[4] The parable implies that he will be judged; his enjoyment in this life will be reversed in the next. This is a Lukan theme in several places. The judgment isn't arbitrary, however, for the man has become a shadow of what he once was. He lives only and always for himself and has no concern for the larger human community—for the welfare, flourishing, and joy of others. He is obsessed with his own fortunes alone and has, in fact, forgotten about God entirely—he "is not rich toward God" (Luke 12:21).

Another way of putting this is that God separates from himself those who have no desire, love, or affection for him. Yes, God punishes, but it is also true that the rich man had chosen his own destiny and his own god, and that god didn't deliver him on the day that death arrived. Luke circles in the same orbit when he says that the proud are scattered, rulers are dismantled, and the rich deprived (Luke 1:51–53). They aren't treated in this way because they are powerful or rich but because of what they have done with their power and riches, using them to oppress and mistreat others. A window is opened onto the state of affairs when they are identified as "proud" (Luke 1:51), which is another way of saying that they have forgotten God, exalting themselves so that God is not their treasure and pleasure.

4 See "ἀπαιτέω," in BDAG 96.

Judgment belongs to those who deny Jesus in the presence of others; they in turn will be denied by Jesus before God (Matt. 10:33; Luke 12:9). The verdict may seem harsh, but it makes perfect sense and accords with justice. We might hope at some moments that decisions in life weren't consequential, as if life had a fantasy-like quality. At our better moments, however, we know and relish the truth that our lives are significant and that what we choose to do with them is momentous.[5] Denying Jesus contradicts the bedrock reality in the universe, the truth that God has revealed about himself. Another way of putting it is that Jesus lets stand the decisions human beings have made about him. He ratifies and confirms the choices we have made about him on the final day, and he judges accordingly.[6]

Eternal Destruction

Judgment is described in destructive terms, and the term "fire" is particularly prominent and fitting to express such, though other expressions are also used to denote devastation. I will argue as well in this section that the judgment represents eternal conscious punishment.

In the parable of the weeds and the wheat, the weeds will be burned at the harvest (Matt. 13:30), representing the destruction of the wicked on the day of judgment. The weeds are aligned with the devil and are his children (Matt. 13:38)—they are the offspring of the serpent (Gen. 3:15; cf. John 8:44). The harvest—the time when the weeds are burned—represents "the end of the age" (Matt. 13:39–40), and at that time those who are "law-breakers" (Matt. 13:41) will be consumed by fire. It should immediately be noted that the image isn't necessarily literal, giving us a picture and illustration of destruction. Commenting on Matthew 3:12, John Calvin points out that the language of fire must be metaphorical:

5   Morris, *The Biblical Doctrine of Judgment,* 51–53, emphasizes that we choose judgment by our own decisions.
6   Though there are some deficiencies in C. S. Lewis's understanding of everlasting judgment, he rightly says, "There are only two kinds of people in the end: those who say to God, 'Thy will be done,' and those to whom God says, in the end, '*Thy* will be done.' All that are in Hell, choose it. Without that self-choice there could be no Hell." C. S. Lewis, *The Great Divorce* (New York: HarperCollins, 2001), 75.

I know there have been many ingenious arguments by many people, but we may gather from many passages of Scripture that is a metaphorical expression; if it were a real and material fire, as they say, one must also agree that the *sulphur* and *blowing* are material, which are mentioned in Isaiah 30.33. Fire is to be understood in the same way as *worm*, for by general agreement the word *worm* is used as a metaphor, to be taken in the same sense as fire.[7]

On Matthew 25:41, he writes,

The word *fire* metaphorically foreshadows the harshness of punishment which passes beyond our understanding. It is totally superfluous ingenuity to inquire, with the sophists, into the matter or form of this fire. By the same reckoning we would ask about the worm, which Isaiah associated with the fire (Isa. 66:24 and 30:33). This author shows plainly in another passage that the expression is metaphorical. He compares the Spirit of God to a fan by which the fire is blown up, and sulphur too is added. These terms make us understand the future vengeance of God upon the wicked, more awful than all the torments of earth, which should strike us more with terror than any desire for research.[8]

The Baptist also warns of "the wrath to come" (Luke 3:7), saying that trees not producing fruit will be thrust into the fire (Luke 3:9; cf. Matt. 3:10). In Matthew, the judgment is compared to chaff that is burned with fire (Matt. 3:12). Fire can be purifying, but here it is clearly a picture of judgment, since those plunged into fire experience destruction. The chaff is not preserved but utterly destroyed. The judgment is also retributive since it is directed against those who don't "bear good fruit" (Matt. 3:10), those who don't "bear fruits in keeping with repentance"

---

7   John Calvin, *Calvin's Commentaries: A Harmony of the Gospels Matthew, Mark and Luke*, ed. D. W. Torrance and T. F. Torrance, trans. A. W. Morrison and T. H. L. Parker (Grand Rapids, MI: Eerdmans, 1972), 1:129.

8   Calvin, *Matthew, Mark and Luke*, 3:117.

(Luke 3:8). Similarly, in Matthew 7:19 trees that don't "bear good fruit" will be axed and cast into the fire. The judgment isn't arbitrary, therefore, but fits with what human beings have done.

A common term for fiery judgment is "hell," a translation of the Greek term *geenna*. The term comes from the "Valley of Hinnom," which became a place where people burned children as sacrifices (Josh. 15:8; 2 Kings 23:10; 2 Chron. 33:6; Jer. 7:31, 32). Along the same lines, 1 Enoch 54:1 speaks of "a valley, deep and burning with fire." The New Testament picks up the notion of a fiery judgment so that the term "hell" (*geenna*) represents the final judgment.[9] For instance, Jesus speaks of "being sentenced to hell" (Matt. 23:33), and wherever the word "hell" is used, the notion of fire is present. We saw earlier that those who are unrighteously angry are subject to final judgment (Matt. 5:21–26) and that judgment is portrayed as "the hell of fire" (*tēn geennan tou pyros*, Matt. 5:22). Similarly, those who don't conquer lust will be thrown into hell (Matt. 5:29, 30). Losing physical life is difficult, but it is far worse to experience future punishment in hell.

Jesus warns about introducing offenses and stumbling blocks into the lives of the little ones who have put their faith in him (Matt. 18:6–7). Using metaphorical language reminiscent of Matthew 5:29–30, he goes on to say that it is better to cut off hands or feet or to gouge out an eye than to let sin get a foothold because, if one allows sin to dominate, one is cast "into the eternal fire" (Matt. 18:8) or "the hell of fire [*tēn geennan tou pyros*]" (Matt 18:9; cf. Mark 9:45, 47). It is obvious that "eternal fire" (*to pyr to aiōnion*) and "hell of fire" describe the same reality. The parallel in Mark describes hell as "the unquenchable fire" (Mark 9:43).

Jesus describes hell as the place "where their worm does not die and the fire is not quenched" (Mark 9:48), picking up on the last verse of the book of Isaiah.[10] The righteous "shall go out and look on the dead bodies of the men who have rebelled against me. For their worm shall not die, their fire shall not be quenched, and they shall be an abhorrence to all

---

9   See Travis, *Christ and the Judgement of God*, 234.

10 Against Travis, *Christ and the Judgement of God*, 235, the text most naturally refers to eternal conscious punishment.

flesh" (Isa. 66:24). Fire denotes final judgment, a judgment that endures forever, and viewing that judgment functions as a warning to the godly.

Describing future punishment as fiery or as an undying worm denotes judgment that is painful and agonizing. In that sense, it could be put into the next category, that of anguish. In saying that fire is a form of destruction, I am not suggesting that the future punishment annihilates human beings. Fire destroys, but it is also painful, and the metaphors should not be pressed unduly. Still, the reference to "eternal fire" suggests that the fire is eternal, that the punishment doesn't end. Some think "eternal" fire means eternal in terms of its effect, but it is more natural to think that the fire itself is eternal, since the punishment is eternal.[11] Similarly, the undying worm and the unquenchable fire are plainly hyperbole, but they most likely denote a state of affairs where punishment doesn't end. Hell is clearly postmortem, and people should fear the one who has the ability to throw one's body and soul into hell (Matt. 10:28; Luke 12:5). If we put this text together with Matthew 18:8–9, the judgment of hell is weightier than physical death, since the punishment never ends. The clearest text on this matter is in Matthew 25. Those who face final judgment are "cursed"; they will be thrown "into the eternal fire prepared for the devil and his angels" (Matt. 25:41). The phrase "eternal fire" surfaces once again. Matthew 25:46 is even more illuminating: "And these will go away into eternal punishment, but the righteous into eternal life." The sheep who have cared for Jesus's brothers and sisters (Matt. 25:40) will enjoy life eternal, while the goats who didn't care for Jesus's family members will suffer eternal punishment.

We should note again that the judgment and punishment accord with the life lived, with what people have done. Thus, the punishment is retributive so that it accords with the behavior and actions of human beings. We also have further evidence that the punishment awarded to those who practiced evil lasts forever. The parallel in Matthew 25:46

---

11 Jerry L. Walls, "A Hell and Purgatory Response," in *Four Views on Hell,* ed. Preston Sprinkle, 2nd ed., Counterpoints (Grand Rapids, MI: Zondervan Academic, 2016), 96–97, rightly says that the traditional view of hell should be accepted unless there are compelling reasons to think otherwise. I dissent, however, from Walls's endorsement of purgatory.

leads us to that conclusion.[12] The righteous enjoy "eternal life," but the wicked are destined for "eternal punishment" (cf. "eternal fire" in Matt. 25:41). Just as eternal life is conscious, so too eternal punishment is conscious.[13] There is no reason to think that the two should be segregated from one another, as if eternal punishment signifies annihilation while eternal life conscious joy that lasts forever. If one supports annihilation as the biblical view, one is in the awkward position of saying that in the case of judgment, "eternal" refers to a punishment that is eternal in consequences but not in consciousness, while eternal life is "eternal" in *both* consequences *and* consciousness. Such a reading is possible but quite unlikely. A more natural reading is that eternal has the same meaning in both clauses.

The notion that future punishment is conscious and unending is also supported by the parable of the rich man and Lazarus where the rich man is in agony in flames (Luke 16:24). Of course, the text can't be pushed too hard since it is a parable. At the same time, we may make the mistake of reading too little out of parables since they open windows that cohere with what we are taught elsewhere. For instance, the portrait of the rich man suffering in flames fits with the notion that there is conscious punishment after death, even if there may not be a literal fire. Jesus sheds light on one dimension of future existence, though we should not press the details to conclude that there is conversation

12 See Scot McKnight, "Eternal Consequences or Eternal Consciousness?," in *Through No Fault of Their Own? The Fate of Those Who Have Never Heard*, ed. William V. Crockett and James G. Sigountos (Grand Rapids, MI: Baker, 1991), 147–57; J. I. Packer, "The Problem of Eternal Punishment," in *The J. I. Packer Collection*, ed. Alister E. McGrath (Leicester, UK: Inter-Varsity Press, 1999), 215.

13 For a robust defense of this position, see Robert A. Peterson, *Hell on Trial: The Case for Eternal Punishment* (Phillipsburg, NJ: Presbyterian & Reformed, 1995). See also Christopher W. Morgan and Robert A. Peterson, eds., *Hell under Fire: Modern Scholarship Reinvents Eternal Punishment* (Grand Rapids, MI: Zondervan Academic, 2004). The biblical argument for eternal punishment goes back to Augustine. See Dongsun Cho, *St. Augustine's Doctrine of Eternal Punishment: His Biblical and Theological Argument* (Lewiston, NY: Edwin Mellen, 2010). Cho shows that Augustine's teaching on eternal punishment did not come from Platonic philosophy but from biblical exegesis and theological reflection. For an excellent popular-level treatment, see Dane Ortlund, *Is Hell Real?*, Church Questions (Wheaton, IL: Crossway, 2022).

between those in heaven and those in hell. The rich man doesn't cease to exist but continues to suffer. Another feature of this account should be noted. There is a clear recognition that both the rich man and Lazarus are receiving the reward deserved. The rich man's callous disregard for Lazarus and for the poor in general demonstrates that his punishment is warranted, that his punishment is retributive.

Another text that points in the direction of unending, conscious punishment is the judgment of Judas, where a woe is pronounced on him for his betrayal of Jesus. Jesus adds that "it would have been better for that man if he had not been born" (Matt. 26:24; cf. Luke 22:22). These words imply that punishment is eternal and can't be limited to annihilation. After all, not being born and annihilation capture the same state of affairs: non-existence. But if it is better for Judas not to be born, we have a hint that his future suffering is conscious and permanent. An annihilationist could reply that it would be better if Judas weren't born since he wasted his life. He could have lived forever, and he threw away that opportunity. On this reading we are faced with the prospect of Judas realizing for a very short time that his life was wasted—only a matter of hours in fact. Thus, on the annihilationist scheme, Judas's consciousness of the gravity of his treachery and its consequences is quite limited.[14] This reading is technically possible but highly improbable. It seems more likely that it would have been better for Judas not to be born because the consequences of his malfeasance endure forever.

Judgment as destruction is pictured in other ways as well. The wicked are those who have built their houses on the foundation of evil (Matt. 7:24–27; Luke 6:46–49), and their houses will collapse with a mighty crash (Matt. 7:27; Luke 6:49). The retributive character of what occurred is again patent. The house implodes because the foundation was flawed, because the materials put into it did not provide stability and ballast. The evil practiced had deleterious consequences, undermining the entire structure.

---

14 Some annihilationists argue that suffering lasts for some time after death and then the wicked are annihilated, and if one holds such a view, the case being made here is lessened. Still, the evidence for a period of punishment before annihilation is scarcely clear.

The word "destroy" (*apollymi*) is used in the parable of the vineyard (Mark 12:9; Luke 20:16), describing the destiny of the vineyard workers who reject the vineyard owner's son. Luke goes on to say that the cornerstone, Jesus the Christ, will break and shatter any who oppose him (Luke 20:18). The same word reflects the fear of demons when they encounter Jesus (Mark 1:24; Luke 4:34). The demons are keenly aware of their ultimate destiny, of their final unraveling, so to speak. Jesus also uses the word "destroy" or "perish" (*apollymi*) twice in Luke 13, as he reflects on the fate of the Galileans whose blood was mingled with sacrifices by Pilate and on the death of the eighteen upon whom the tower of Siloam fell (Luke 13:3, 5). Such tragedies during this life anticipate and point to a far greater calamity. Those who fail to repent and turn from their sin will be destroyed on the last day. The catastrophes in this world function as warnings and reminders that life isn't trivial, that a day of judgment impends, a day when some will perish. Jesus isn't suggesting that those who die in earthly disasters will also necessarily perish on the last day. He says that such events are parables, instructing us to be prepared for the judgment to come.

Anguish

The punishment that follows judgment is also described in terms of personal anguish, where there is profound and everlasting regret. Those judged are hurled into "outer darkness" and experience "weeping and gnashing of teeth" (Matt. 8:12; 22:13; 25:30; see also Matt. 13:42, 50; 24:51; Luke 13:28). Some ethnic Jews, who are children of the covenant, will be filled with regret and anger as they see Gentiles enjoying the messianic feast with Abraham, Isaac, and Jacob while they themselves are excluded (Matt. 8:10–12; Luke 13:28–29). The anger ("gnashing of teeth"—cf. Job 16:9; Pss. 35:16; 37:12; 112:10; Lam. 2:16; Acts 7:54) points to a continued unrepentant heart and an ongoing hatred of God. It seems that the experience at the final judgment accords with what we read in Proverbs 19:3:

> When a man's folly brings his way to ruin,
> his heart rages against the LORD.

So there isn't only sorrow and pain but also rage, a rage directed against God himself.

Weeping and gnashing of teeth is also the destiny of those who will be thrown into a fiery furnace (Matt. 13:42, 50). The man lacking a wedding garment is cast into the outer darkness, where he will weep and gnash his teeth (Matt. 22:11–13). The outer darkness represents terror since one feels helpless in the dark and may stumble to destruction.

Furthermore, enemies lurk in the darkness and may pounce at any moment in the gloom of night. Of course, these are metaphors of the future judgment, and outer darkness functions as another metaphor in the same way that fiery destruction is a metaphor. Darkness and fire don't coexist, and so we recognize that the descriptions aren't literal. Saying that the images are metaphorical doesn't lead to the conclusion that the punishment is illusory. The punishment is real but is expressed metaphorically, and the metaphor of darkness points to the desolation, the fear, the lostness that the wicked will experience. John Piper remarks, "Do people use symbols of horror because the reality is less horrible or more horrible than the symbols? I don't know of anyone who uses symbolic language for horrible realities when literal language would make it sound more horrible."[15] Similarly, Calvin says, "Because no description can deal adequately with the gravity of God's vengeance against the wicked, their torments and tortures are figuratively expressed to us by physical things. . . . By such expressions the Holy Spirit certainly intended to confound all our senses with dread."[16]

The judgment of the man without the wedding garment is rendered since he clearly doesn't belong at the final wedding feast. The point of the illustration is that only those who truly belong to the Lord will be in his presence. The punishment fits the crime, just as it makes no sense to show up at a beautiful wedding with gym shorts and a torn

15 John Piper, "God's Wrath: 'Vengeance Is Mine, I will Repay,'" Desiring God, February 27, 2005, https://www.desiringgod.org/.

16 John Calvin, *Institutes of the Christian Religion*, ed. John T. McNeill, trans. Ford Lewis Battles, 2 vols., LCC (Philadelphia: Westminster, 1960), 2:1007 (3.25.12).

T-shirt. Along the same lines, Jesus paints the picture of a household servant responsible for the household (Matt. 24:45–51). If the servant is responsible, he will be rewarded. On the other hand, if he abuses fellow servants and gets drunk, the master will "cut him in pieces" and place him with "hypocrites" in a place of "weeping and gnashing of teeth" (Matt. 24:51). Similarly, servants who hide their talents instead of investing them will be cast "into the outer darkness" where "there will be weeping and gnashing of teeth" (Matt. 25:30).

Demons recognize that future punishment involves pain when they ask if Jesus has come "to torment" (*basanizō*) them before the final day of judgment (Matt. 8:29), signaling that the day of judgment will bring excruciating distress. The noun "tormentor" (*basanistēs*) is used to describe the torture the person will experience who refuses to forgive his brother or sister from his heart (Matt. 18:34–35).

The Greco-Roman world was an honor-shame society, and the final judgment is portrayed as a day when the Son of Man will be ashamed of those who were ashamed of him (Luke 9:26). The implication is that those punished will be ashamed since they will be rejected on that great day. The shame they feel is clearly retributive—the Son of Man expresses shame over them because they are ashamed of him. Those who belong to the Lord are blessed now and in the eschaton (Matt. 5:3–12; Luke 6:20–23). Conversely, those who are separated from God will experience eschatological woes so that those who are rich now will suffer, those who are full now will be hungry, those who laugh now will mourn, and those who are popular now will be excluded (Luke 6:24–26). A great reversal, a profound turning, is coming—and there is no doubt about the impending justice. Instead, it is evident that people receive what they deserve, that the scales of justice will finally be set right.

The Gospel of John

John's Gospel stands out for its emphasis on realized eschatology, which means that the realities of the age to come have arrived in this present evil age. John's realized eschatology emerges when he speaks of judgment as well. Thus, in John 3:18 those who don't believe in Jesus as God's Son are "condemned already." The verb "condemned" is perfect tense (*kekritai*), signifying a reality that is present. The present reality of judgment is emphasized further by the use of the word "already" (*ēdē*). Condemnation is an existing reality for those who refuse to believe in the Son who came to save the world, the one who came so that people would not "perish" (*apolētai*) in the final judgment (John 3:16–17). According to John, the world needs saving, but it stands to reason that those who reject the one who came to save stand under judgment. John expands on the judgment in John 3:19–20, explaining why people refuse to come to the light that has dawned with the coming of Jesus (cf. also John 1:9; 8:12). People flee from the light because of the evil they practice: they don't want the light to expose the wickedness of their behavior. Judgment belongs to those who don't want to admit to reality and to the truth. They insist on hiding their evil to avoid shame (even though admitting and forsaking their sin is the path to freedom), but they also veil their actions so that they can continue to practice evil. John emphasizes here that paradoxically some human beings choose darkness and judgment when an opportunity for salvation and truth is opened to them.

John 3:36 strikes similar chords. In John 3:31–36, Jesus brings heavenly testimony, a transcendent word as the one sent by the Father. He has spoken a true word, but human beings have rejected the testimony, though those who believe in the Son of God have eternal life now. The one who disobeys and disbelieves (*apeithōn*) will not enjoy life (John 3:36). Instead, "the wrath of God remains [*menei*] on him." The word "remains" points to the present experience of wrath that they stand under even during this life. Here the judgment stems from the refusal to hear a word above and beyond us, a heavenly word, a word about the Son to whom the Father has given everything. Conversely, those who hear Jesus's message, believing in the Father who sent him, have eternal life now; they will avoid the coming judgment and have already "passed [*metabebēken*] from death to life" (John 5:24).

John doesn't reserve judgment or salvation to the present age but also speaks of a future judgment. As the Son of Man, Jesus is granted the right to pass judgment (John 5:27). John reaches back to Daniel 7 where the Son of Man is given the kingdom by the Ancient of Days (Dan. 7:13–14), and as the corporate head of the saints he will convene a court and judge the world (Dan. 7:26–27). John envisions the day when the court will be in session, when tombs are opened, when those who have practiced what is good are raised to life while those who have indulged in evil are raised for final condemnation (John 5:28–29). It is evident that the judgment is retributive, that it accords with what people do, and thus it is fair, equitable, just, and sensible.

Later, Jesus warns those who resisted his teaching that Moses will join in the accusation against them on the last day, because they didn't believe in Jesus. Such unbelief is indefensible since Moses wrote about Jesus (John 5:45–47), and they claim to treasure and believe in Moses's writings. The various witnesses that testify to Jesus come to the forefront in John 5. They include the Baptist (John 5:31–35), Jesus's works (John 5:36), the Father himself (John 5:37), and the Scriptures (John 5:38–39), which also includes the writings of Moses (John 5:45–47). From the presence of so many witnesses to the truth that is in Jesus, we can draw the following: there is ample reason for the final judgment, since the evidence for believing in Jesus is incontrovertible. Those who disbelieve have no excuse for their recalcitrance and resistance to Jesus, and their stubbornness shows that they don't love the glory of God but the praise, honor, and good opinion of human beings (John 5:44).

Similar themes are introduced in John 8:12–20. The Pharisees object that Jesus's testimony can't be accepted since he testified about himself. But Jesus countered that his testimony should be believed because he knows both where he came from and his future destiny. The standard of judgment used by his adversaries shouldn't be trusted since they assess matters according to the flesh. By way of contrast, Jesus judges no one, and he probably means by this that he wasn't rendering final judgment on anyone during his ministry. He didn't come to judge the world but to save it (cf. John 3:17). We are reminded of the Old Testament teaching that God is "slow to anger" (Ex. 34:6; Num. 14:18; Neh. 9:17; Pss. 86:15; 103:8; 145:8; Joel 2:13; Jonah 4:2; Nah. 1:3). The Lord's judgment is just but not immediate. He patiently gives people time to repent. Still, if Jesus judges, his judgment is reliable because he and the Father jointly judge.

Jesus then returns to the matter of testimony, claiming that his testimony has credence because it is a testimony that comes from the Father and the Son. The opponents of Jesus didn't receive his testimony since they didn't know the Father or the Son. Jesus's judgment doesn't merely accord with human standards or conceptions, which are fallible, limited, and partial. His judgment accords with the truth since it is a divine judgment, a judgment coauthored by the Father and the Son. Here is a judgment that sees the whole metanarrative and encompasses all reality. Such a judgment is impossible for mere human beings, but Jesus's judgment isn't merely human, so his judgment accords with reality, with the truth. Thus, there is no question about whether the judgment is unfair. The judgment is just because it takes into account all the facts of the case.

At first glance, John 9:39 seems to contradict John 3:17. In the latter Jesus says he didn't come to condemn the world, but the former says that he came to judge the world. Such paradoxes, however, characterize John's writing, and when we look closer, we see that there isn't truly a contradiction. When Jesus says that he came to save the world, the reference is to his explicit intention and motivation for coming into the world. He is slow to anger! Judgment wasn't his fundamental motivation for entering the world but the inevitable consequence or result of his coming. Thus, Jesus came so that those who are blind would come to see (John 9:39). Those who continue in their blindness, claiming that they see clearly, are those who refuse to receive the testimony about Jesus. They would not persist in their blindness if they humbled themselves and acknowledged their sin. Judgment belongs to those who proclaim their own righteousness, who are too prideful to plead to Jesus for forgiveness, and who persist in evil.

Thus, Jesus didn't intentionally come to judge—that was not his *raison d'etre*—but judgment is the destiny and consequence for those who don't ask for forgiveness.

We find a similar text in John 12:47–50, where Jesus says that he refrains from judging those who fail to keep his words since he didn't "come to judge the world but to save the world" (John 12:47). At first glance this seems to say that there will be no judgment for the disobedient. But John's paradoxical style surfaces again since in the next verse (John 12:48), Jesus says that there will be judgment for the one who rejects him and his teaching: "The word that I have spoken will judge him on the last day." We see again that Jesus's primary aim wasn't to judge but to save. Furthermore, he doesn't judge during this age since this is the era of salvation. His word will judge on the last day. There is a judgment coming, but the present *aeon* is a time for repentance and belief, for salvation and deliverance from wrath. Jesus affirms in John 12:49–50 that he speaks as the Father who sent him commanded. The final judgment has divine authorization so that the word of judgment Jesus will speak on the last day is a divine word. At the same time, Jesus came fundamentally to save. We have the recognition that judgment is the Lord's strange and foreign work (Isa. 28:21), that his fundamental desire is to save not to destroy.

Conclusion

We learn from the Gospels and Acts that Jesus often spoke about the judgment. The coming judgment is a verdict that will be announced on the last day against the wicked. This verdict is not an empty one since those who are judged will experience destruction and anguish, dissolution and unending pain. The images used for destruction, such as the reference to fire, should not be pressed as if they physically describe what will happen. On the other hand, the judgment is *real and eternal*. The metaphors point to a judgment that means the unraveling of human life, a torment that is unending. In the Gospel of John, those who don't believe will be judged, face God's wrath, and be cut off from the life that God gives. It is imperative to remember that all the texts about judgment in the Gospels and Acts are intended to provoke people to repent. God is merciful to those who repent; he doesn't judge immediately. People are warned of the hurricane that is coming so that they will take shelter in Christ before the storm arrives. At the same time, the rightness and justice of the judgment is underscored. No one is judged unfairly; all those who are judged deserve it.

Judgment in the Epistles

*But because of your hard and impenitent heart you
are storing up wrath for yourself on the day of wrath
when God's righteous judgment will be revealed.*

Introduction

We have seen that judgment was a critical element of Jesus's preaching
and a common theme in the Gospels and Acts. The same is true in the
Pauline Epistles and the General Epistles. The presence of this theme
in the epistles supports the notion that judgment is a pervasive theme
in the Scriptures. In this chapter, I will consider how both contribute
to the biblical view of God's judgment.

Pauline Epistles

Key Texts

Brendan Byrne says that "the motif of the last judgment is an essential
element of the apocalyptic horizon against which the entire economy
of salvation according to Paul must be understood."[1] Paul features the

---

1   Brendan Byrne, *Paul and the Economy of Salvation: Reading from the Perspective of the
     Last Judgment* (Grand Rapids, MI: Baker Academic, 2021), 1–2. See esp. 43–172, where

gospel in his writings, where he unpacks the good news that saves sinners from the judgment to come. We grasp the riches of our salvation when we gain a clear understanding of how judgment is warranted. Separating the different dimensions of judgment in Paul is somewhat artificial, and the categories overlap. We will begin by looking at two key texts on judgment in Romans 2 and 2 Thessalonians 1. In the discussion of Romans 2, I will consider some additional verses that contribute to the theme. Then I will turn to texts that speak of (1) God's judgment and (2) the consequences of his wrath and judgment—that is, death, perishing, not inheriting the kingdom, and so on.

Romans 2 is a key passage on God's judgment. Those who judge others "condemn" (*katakrineis*) themselves since they engage in the same evils that they criticize in others (Rom. 2:1). A superficial reading might lead us to think that condemnation comes from judging, but actually judgment is threatened for those who judge others for their evil *while doing the same things themselves.* Paul affirms that God's "judgment" (*krima*) accords with the truth for those who *practice evil* (Rom. 2:2), which means that the judgment of God accords with reality, with the true nature of things, assuring us that God judges rightly. God's patience and forbearance is emphasized, certifying that his desire is for all people to repent and to avoid judgment (Rom. 2:4). Because of God's great love, he warns people of the judgment to come so that they will take steps to avoid it. Still, those whose hearts are stubborn, those who refuse to turn from sin, are storing up for themselves wrath on the day God pours out his wrath (cf. Rom. 1:18), and they will experience God's "righteous judgment" (*dikaiokrisias*, Rom. 2:5).

God's judgment isn't arbitrary but righteous, a judgment that is deserved by those who resist his kind and gracious overtures of mercy. His wrath is directed against godlessness and unrighteousness since people clearly know God's will but gladly give themselves over to idolatry instead of serving and loving the one true God (Rom. 1:18–25). God's

Byrne thoroughly canvasses many texts on the last judgment in Paul. See also the important work of John R. Coulson, *The Righteous Judgment of God: Aspects of Judgment in Paul's Letters* (Eugene, OR: Wipf & Stock, 2016).

wrath is an expression of his justice, and ultimately it is an eschatological phenomenon. Currently the fullness of God's wrath is hidden from the world, but it will be unveiled on the final day.

Romans 2:6–11 expands on God's righteous judgment, and the thesis statement is presented in 2:6: God judges every person in accord with their works (cf. 2 Cor. 11:15; Col. 3:25).[2] Romans 2:7–10 are a chiasm that unpack 2:6:

a   Those who do good will receive eternal life (2:7)
   b   God's wrath and anger will be poured out on those who practice evil (2:8)
   b′ People who practice evil will experience tribulation and distress (2:9)
a′ God will give glory, honor, and peace to those who do what is good (2:10)

The focus in this book is on judgment, and thus we will concentrate on Romans 2:8–9, where judgment is the subject. God's punishment is active and direct in that those who do evil will be on the receiving end of God's wrath (Rom. 2:8). We already saw a reference to God's wrath in Romans 2:5, and there is a logical connection between Romans 2:6–11 and Romans 2:5. The relationship between the two is quite simple: God's righteous judgment and wrath will be poured out on the those who practice evil, and he will reward those who do what is good. Paul confirms in other texts as well that God will display his wrath on the final day.

We see in Ephesians 5:5–6 and Colossians 3:5–6 that those who are disobedient and give themselves to wickedness will face God's wrath eschatologically. The punishment is clearly retributive since the wrath comes from God and is the destiny of those who disobey.[3]

2   Surprisingly, Stephen H. Travis, *Christ and the Judgement of God: The Limits of Divine Retribution in New Testament Thought* (Peabody, MA: Hendrickson, 2009), says that wrath isn't retributive in this text, but Rom. 2:6 shows the opposite—the consequences of sin represent God's repayment of their sin.
3   Travis, *Christ and the Judgement of God*, 69, says it isn't retributive but depends on whether one is in Christ. But in saying this, he introduces a false dichotomy. He rightly avers that

Conversely, those who belong to Jesus will be rescued from the wrath that is coming (1 Thess. 1:10), since Jesus by his death took the wrath they deserved.[4] Thus, believers are not appointed to wrath but for final salvation (1 Thess. 5:9). Wrath in Romans 5:9 stands in contrast to justification, and Stephen Travis rightly says that wrath takes place in the context of a relationship with God, but he strays in saying that wrath isn't retributive.[5] Retribution and personal response to sin should not be separated from one another.[6] Indeed, C. S. Lewis rightly opines, in a famous essay, that judgment is only just and right if it is retributive.[7]

God's wrath isn't whimsical but is directed against all that is wrong and twisted in the world. Unbelievers are dead in their sins and offenses, and sin's hold is multifaceted so that it shows up psychologically (they desire evil), sociologically (they are influenced by society), and spiritually (they are under the devil's authority, Eph. 2:1–3). Indeed, all human beings come into the world as "children of wrath" (Eph. 2:3), as those deserving eschatological punishment. Since human beings lack spiritual life, the law, representing God's will and ways, doesn't solve the human dilemma since the law doesn't transform human beings but produces transgression (Rom. 4:15). The consequence of such transgression is God's wrath.

We ought not say that God is by nature full of wrath, as if wrath is an attribute of God. Instead, his wrath is an expression of his justice, rep-

---

salvation in Christ is free and not a matter of recompense, but he doesn't tie this free salvation to Christ taking the judgment of God on our behalf. Furthermore, even though salvation is free and unmerited, judgment is just and merited. One of the root problems of Travis's reading (see 69–70) is the claim that there can't be wrath where there are personal relationships. Such a claim, however, is imposed on the text from the outside. We have a both-and here instead of an either-or. Wrath is retributive *and* manifested in personal relationships.

4   See here Byrne, *Paul and the Economy of Salvation*, 48. Travis, *Christ and the Judgement of God*, 56–57, again wrongly inserts a wedge between relationship and retribution, seeing the wrath as the former but not the latter.

5   Travis, *Christ and the Judgement of God*, 64.

6   The same could be said for Christopher D. Marshall (*Beyond Retribution: A New Testament Vision for Justice, Crime, and Punishment* [Grand Rapids, MI: Eerdmans, 2001], 35–95, 122–24), who tends to set the covenant over against retributive judgment.

7   C. S. Lewis, "The Humanitarian Theory of Punishment," *Churchman* 73 (1959): 55–60.

resenting his response to human sin. God avenges sin (Rom. 12:19–20; 1 Thess. 4:6) since he is just and holy and good.[8] God's wrath can also be described as jealousy (1 Cor. 10:22). Although the latter is typically understood to be a negative emotion, God is jealous for the truth—for reality as it is. But the worship of demons or idols (1 Cor. 10:21) distorts and misleads so that the true God isn't worshiped, praised, and adored.

The discussion on wrath brings us back to Romans 2. On the one hand, those who sin and fail to repent, those who refuse to turn back to God, experience his wrath. If we look at the judgment in terms of human experience, those who practice evil face tribulation and distress (Rom. 2:9). Sin brings anguish, misery, and pain, and in this context such misery is clearly eschatological.

Annihilationists contend that this misery and pain is short-lived since the wicked are put out of existence. But such a reading, though possible, is not convincing. The reference to misery and anguish make more sense if it lasts more than a brief moment before one is annihilated. It is more likely, then, that Paul describes psychological torment that isn't temporary but enduring, referring to an eternal and ongoing anguish. Such a prospect causes some to question God's justice, and yet Paul, if I am interpreting him correctly, posits such a future in a context that affirms God's *righteous* judgment.

Romans 2:11 also plays an important function in the argument. Romans 2:6–11 affirm that God judges according to works, and 2:11 provides the basis or ground for that claim. God judges by works because he is fair and impartial, refusing to play favorites. It could scarcely be clearer. Paul doesn't believe that God's judgment of both the righteous and the wicked causes us to question God's justice. Quite the contrary. God's judgment displays and vindicates his justice—it verifies that God

---

8   Cf. Coulson, *The Righteous Judgment of God*, 69. Not every reference to wrath in Paul refers to the final eschaton. God responds to human sin with wrath according to Rom. 1:18, and as a consequence he hands human beings over to sin (Rom. 1:24, 26, 28). The handing over to sin may culminate in experiencing the end-time wrath of God, but the handing over to sin in Rom. 1 should not be construed to say that those who are handed over will inevitably face final judgment. While life remains, they may repent and turn from sin and experience salvation.

is good and impartial and righteous. The eternal punishment of the wicked doesn't call into question God's justice; it verifies and supports it.

One of the most significant texts on God's judgment is 2 Thessalonians 1:5–9. Paul refers to God's "righteous judgment" (*dikaias kriseōs*, 1:5), and then contends that it is "just" (*dikaion*, 1:6) for God to repay those who mistreat believers. The formulation is interesting because for God to do nothing in this situation, allowing unbelievers to afflict believers without any punishment, would be unjust and unfair, according to Paul. The repayment for unbelievers will occur at the eschaton, when Jesus along with his mighty angels is revealed from heaven at his return (2 Thess. 1:7), and thus the punishment doesn't occur during this life. On that day, "vengeance" (*ekdikēsin*) will be meted out not only to those who mistreat believers but also to those who don't know God and to those who refuse to submit to the gospel of Christ (2 Thess. 1:8). The "punishment" (*dikēn*) imposed will be "eternal destruction" (*olethron aiōnion*) so that they are removed from the Lord's gracious presence and from his glorious might (2 Thess. 1:9). Paul envisions eternal punishment as the recompense for those who reject the gospel and for those who don't know God (cf. 1 Cor. 5:12–13).

Denny Burk rightly argues that when unbelievers are separated from God's presence and power, it doesn't mean that they cease to exist. Instead, Paul's point is that they are cut off eternally from the mercy of Christ and experience God's wrath forever.[9] Travis attempts to downplay the retributive element by saying that Paul uses traditional language and doesn't buy into the notion of recompense,[10] but there is no reason to think that Paul doesn't embrace the tradition of *lex talionis* (the law of retaliation) since he uses it extensively here. What's more, Paul emphasizes that such punishment is just, right, and fair. The many words with roots of the term *righteousness* (*dik-*) in this text impress upon readers the justice of the retribution. The words "eternal

9   Denny Burk, "Eternal Conscious Torment," in *Four Views on Hell*, ed. Preston Sprinkle, 2nd ed., Counterpoints (Grand Rapids, MI: Zondervan Academic, 2016), 34–35.

10 Travis, *Christ and the Judgement of God*, 76–79.

destruction" could be construed in terms of annihilation, but it seems more plausible (as noted above) that unbelievers are eternally and consciously removed from his merciful presence. In other words, they aren't cut off from Christ's presence by being blotted out of existence. What unbelievers will experience is exclusion from Christ's gracious presence, and the punishment is particularly grievous because they are fully aware of what they are missing. Warnings of judgment have a salutary effect. R. V. G. Tasker rightly says, "To realize that we are under God's wrath and in disgrace is the essential preliminary to the experience of His love and grace."[11] Those who fail to repent in this life will not experience God's love in the next.

God's Judgment

We turn next to texts that speak of God and/or Christ as Judge. Paul proclaims that at Jesus's appearing, on the day the kingdom is consummated, he will "judge the living and the dead" (2 Tim. 4:1). The judgment is universal, and no person who lived will escape standing before Christ to render account for their lives. Paul describes the final judgment in Romans 14:12 as a day when "each of us will give an account of himself to God." The wording of 2 Corinthians 5:10 accords with 2 Timothy 4:1: "For we must all appear before the judgment seat of Christ, so that each one may receive what is due for what he has done in the body, whether good or evil." The final judgment is the work of God and Christ: all will be judged, the judgment will be equitable, and each one will be recompensed for what he or she has done.

It isn't my purpose here to work out how judgment according to works fits with justification by faith.[12] I have written on this elsewhere and argued that our works constitute evidence and proof that we are

---

11 R. V. G. Tasker, *The Biblical Doctrine of the Wrath of God* (London: Tyndale Press, 1951), 9.

12 Some have argued that judgment before the *bēma* seat (see Rom. 14:10; 2 Cor. 5:10) relates to rewards, not final judgment. See, e.g., David K. Lowery, "2 Corinthians," in *The Bible Knowledge Commentary: An Exposition of the Scriptures*, ed. J. F. Walvoord and R. B. Zuck (Wheaton, IL: Victor Books, 1985), 566. But it isn't clear that either of these texts refer to rewards. It is more natural, especially in 2 Cor. 5:10—and because of what Paul writes elsewhere—to understand Paul as referring to works that are a necessary evidence

trusting in Christ for salvation, since—apart from the forgiveness of sins and the gift of righteousness offered in the gospel—no one would be vindicated on the final day.[13] Our works can't be the *basis* of our justification since when we look at what we have done as human beings, "every mouth" will be shut and the entire world will be considered guilty (*hypodikos*) before God (Rom. 3:19). Sometimes the word *hypodikos* is translated "accountable," but that translation is misleading since one can be accountable and cleared as innocent, as one may meet the standards for which one is accountable. Rather, the term means "guilty."[14] And the judgment brings fear, since no one keeps God's requirements (cf. Rom. 2:12). "All have sinned and fall short of the glory of God" (Rom. 3:23), and Paul reminds us that no one is righteous before God (Rom. 3:10). Indeed, God judges the *secrets* of people's hearts (Rom. 2:16), which means that he knows the hidden evils we have wrought—in thought, in word, and in deed. Human beings aren't capable of rendering final judgment since our knowledge is partial and limited. We don't know the secret sins lurking in the hearts of others or the secret evils they have carried out.

We are unable to judge fully the motives of others or even our own motives (1 Cor. 4:3–5) since we can't ever know our own motives fully. Only the Lord knows the secrets of the heart and how people have truly lived. Thus, on the day of judgment the Lord will "bring to light the things now hidden in darkness and will disclose the purposes of the heart" (1 Cor. 4:5). We can be assured that the judgment is right since God's understanding is comprehensive and infinite, including the secret things people have done and the motives of the heart.

---

of salvation. See here David E. Garland, *2 Corinthians,* CSC (Nashville: B&H Academic, 2021), 293–95.

13 Thomas R. Schreiner, "Did Paul Believe in Justification by Works? Another Look at Romans 2," *BBR* 3 (1993): 131–58; Thomas R. Schreiner, *Justification: An Introduction,* SSST (Wheaton, IL: Crossway, 2023), 133–40. See also Kevin W. McFadden, *Judgment according to Works in Romans: The Meaning and Function of Divine Judgment in Paul's Most Important Letter,* Emerging Scholars (Minneapolis: Fortress, 2013).

14 Thomas R. Schreiner, *Romans,* 2nd ed., BECNT (Grand Rapids, MI: Baker Academic, 2018), 175.

Romans 3:4–6 is most interesting on the theme of judgment. Every human being is indicted as a liar in the sense that every person turns toward idolatry and self-worship, bowing to the creature rather than the Creator (Rom. 1:18–25). Thus, God is "justified" (*dikaiōthēs*) in his words of judgment, and he will triumph in the judgment (Rom. 3:4). God judges human beings according to the truth of who he is, and that truth is denied by human beings who turn inward toward the self instead of outward toward God. In turning inward, we embrace the lie of human independence, as if we could flourish without God, as if the creature deserves the same praise as the Creator (Rom. 1:25). The truth of judgment brings people back to reality, revealing both the true nature of God and of human beings. Human "unrighteousness" (*adikia*) displays, then, God's "righteousness" (*dikaiosynēn*) in judgment, vindicating God's justice (Rom. 3:5). Otherwise, as Paul says, if judgment is precluded, then there would be no judgment or justice in the world (Rom. 3:6).

In talking about the judgment of the world, Paul addresses the Jews and has in mind particularly the judgment of Gentiles. If the Jews of Paul's day were convinced of anything, it was that Gentiles should be judged! As Morris says about the argument made by Paul, "The final judgment is not something that must be argued for. It is something that may be argued from. Paul assumes that there will be no dispute about this. It is common ground for all Christians."[15] Actually, Paul sees it as common ground for Jews as well, even Jews who don't believe in the gospel. We can take the argument even further and say that Paul's words apply universally. Paul asks us to imagine a world where there is no judgment, no accountability, and no recompense for evils that are done. Such a world is intolerable and senseless, degrading our humanity, since what we do with our lives would be insignificant and have no moral value.[16] Without judgment everything would be permitted, nothing would be verboten, and goodness would vanish into the mists of nothingness.

---

15   Leon Morris, *The Biblical Doctrine of Judgment* (Grand Rapids, MI: Eerdmans, 1960), 55.
16   Coulson, *The Righteous Judgment of God*, 132–33.

God's curse represents his judgment, his verdict against human beings. All those who proclaim a gospel contrary to the Pauline gospel
are cursed (Gal. 1:8–9). The word for "curse" (*anathema*) doesn't refer
to "an act of church discipline in the sense of excommunication; the
curse rather exposes the culprits to the judicial wrath of God himself."[17]
We find the word at the close of the Corinthian letter: "If anyone has no
love for the Lord, let him be accursed" (1 Cor. 16:22). The final eschatological curse is certainly intended since the next words (*marana tha*)
entreat the Lord to return, to come to earth to wrap up all of history.
Being a believer doesn't merely mean that we do what is right, though
it certainly includes such. Those who believe also love the Lord—they
have an affection for him, a longing for him, a desire to be satisfied
with his unfailing love. Another verse that relays the final judgment is
2 Timothy 2:12, where Paul picks up the words of Jesus (Matt. 10:33;
Luke 12:9): "If we deny him, he also will deny us." Paul doesn't use the
language of cursing, but the denial coming from Jesus represents an
eschatological verdict. Those who fully and finally deny Jesus the Christ
will be denied by him on the last day.

Death and Destruction

The consequence of sin is death, and this has been God's verdict since
Adam and Eve transgressed in the garden (Gen. 2:17). Paul affirms
that Adam's sin brought death into the world, and all people—who
are sons and daughters of Adam—die because of sin (Rom. 5:12, 15,
17). Death can't be limited to physical death but also includes final
separation from God. This is confirmed in the context of Romans 5
where death is conjoined in the context with condemnation (Rom.
5:16, 18). It is appropriate, then, to say that death in Paul has two
dimensions, physical death and eternal death. The Mosaic law didn't
transform human hearts, since the letter apart from the Spirit puts
to death (2 Cor. 3:6). Thus, the Mosaic covenant is characterized as
a "ministry of death" (2 Cor. 3:7). This death isn't merely physical

---

17 "*Anathema*," in *NIDNTTE* 1.282.

because the covenant with Moses is also described as a "ministry of condemnation" (2 Cor. 3:9).

A very significant observation on death surfaces in Romans 1:32. Human beings know God's ordinance—that is, they realize that those who give themselves to sin deserve death (*axioi thanatou*). Nevertheless, they continue to give themselves over to sin and encourage others to do so as well. Death here refers both to physical death and eternal death, as was noted above. The punishment is retributive and personal, showing that the judgment isn't arbitrary but corresponds with what people do. What stands out, however, is that all human beings know that sin warrants death, even if they don't have God's written torah. The judgment meted out, therefore, accords with the conscience and intuitions of human beings. Even if human beings suppress the truth, they realize at some level (perhaps deep in their subconscious) that they deserve final punishment. This is not to deny that some may experience a kind of grief and sorrow at the consequences of their sin without truly turning away from sin (2 Cor. 7:10–12). Such "worldly grief produces death" (2 Cor. 7:10), while godly grief and repentance bring life and forgiveness.

Paul often teaches that sin leads to death (Rom. 6:16, 21). He famously declares that "the wages of sin is death" (Rom. 6:23). The image of wages shows that death functions as retribution, as repayment, for the life human beings have lived. Once again, death isn't limited to physical death since it is contrasted with eternal life (Rom. 6:22–23), justifying the conclusion that those who give themselves over to sin will experience eternal death. Travis claims that retribution isn't in view since eternal life isn't retributive,[18] and it is certainly true that eternal life isn't what is deserved but a gift given to us. On the other hand, it seems that eternal death is retributive since Paul *contrasts the gift* of eternal life with the *wages* of sin. Eternal life is free and non-retributive, but death is deserved and retributive. Along the same lines, "to set the mind on the flesh is death" (Rom. 8:6), which means that the mindset

---

18 Travis, *Christ and the Judgement of God*, 82–84.

of the flesh results in or leads to death. The mindset of the flesh results in death since the thinking of unbelievers leads to evil, and evil in turn brings death. Believers are warned that if they give way to the flesh—if they live according to bodily desires, if they let their selfish wills dominate their lives—they will die (Rom. 8:13). Again, death isn't merely physical since it is contrasted with life. Indeed, Paul refers to the future resurrection where those who belong to Christ live forever as those raised from the dead (Rom. 8:11).

In the Pauline letters, the final destiny of those who are judged is often spoken of as perishing or as being destroyed. In some contexts, the word simply refers to physical destruction or death (e.g., 1 Cor. 10:9–10; 2 Cor. 4:9). Often, however, the destruction is clearly eschatological. Paul contrasts, for instance, those who "are being saved" with those "who are perishing" (*apollymenois*, 2 Cor. 2:15), and the contrast demonstrates that those who are perishing are excluded from eschatological salvation. The gospel is veiled "to those who are perishing" (2 Cor. 4:3), and they perish because they don't see the beauty of who Christ is, because God's light hasn't dawned in their hearts (2 Cor. 4:4, 6). Since unbelievers are excluded from seeing the glory and beauty of Christ, the good news about Jesus Christ crucified and risen is "folly" to them, as "those who are perishing" (1 Cor. 1:18). If Christ isn't truly risen from the dead (but of course he has risen!—1 Cor. 15:1–11, 20–22), believers who have fallen asleep (died), have "perished" (1 Cor. 15:18). Clearly, the perishing here represents a further punishment after death, a punishment that belongs to those whose sins aren't forgiven (1 Cor. 15:17).

So, too, the day of the Lord (1 Thess. 5:2; cf. 1 Cor. 5:5) is coming, a day when the righteous will be vindicated and the wicked judged. When it arrives, "sudden destruction" (*aiphnidios . . . olethros*) will be the fate of those living in darkness, of those who are not the children of the light (1 Thess. 5:3–5). It will be a day when a fire, so to speak, tests the lives of all, and those who destroy God's temple, the church of Jesus Christ, will themselves be destroyed (*phtheirei*, 1 Cor. 3:13–17). Similarly, those who oppose the Philippian believers are headed for destruction (*apōleias*), which stands for eschatological ruin since the same verse contrasts the destiny of the opponents with that of the Philippian believers, and the latter are promised salvation (Phil. 1:28). Opponents who oppose Christ and his cross face an "end" (*telos*), an outcome, that is "destruction" (*apōleia*, Phil. 3:18–19). Those who sin without being acquainted with the Mosaic law "will also perish without the law" (Rom. 2:12). Perishing in this context is parallel to being judged, which is the destiny of those who sin while possessing the law (Rom. 2:12). We should not overemphasize the differences between these two expressions, for judgment and perishing both describe eschatological ruin for the wicked.

Eschatology pervades 2 Thessalonians 2, where the coming man of lawlessness and the havoc he will wreak is painted in. Ultimately, Jesus "will kill" him (*anelei*) and "bring [him] to nothing" (*katargēsei*) at his second coming (2 Thess. 2:8). If the man of lawlessness is the same person as the beast in Revelation, which is likely, John describes the same event in terms of the beast being thrown into the lake of fire (Rev. 19:20). Paul goes on to speak of the deceived who are "perishing" (*apollymenois*, 2 Thess. 2:10). They are perishing because they refused to love the truth, and perishing is contrasted with salvation, which they would have received if they had loved and embraced the truth. Since they rejected the truth of the gospel, God sends a spirit of deceit (2 Thess. 2:10–11). On the last day they will stand "condemned" (*krithōsin*) as those who did not give themselves to the truth but instead delighted in and took pleasure in unrighteousness (2 Thess. 2:12). Final judgment is fitting since those who perish embrace and delight in what is false and find the truth repulsive. They rejected Christ in this life, and thus they will be separated from him in the life to come. In that sense, the separation from God they desired will be a reality. God will confirm and ratify their choices, though the anguish they will experience will surprise them.

Paul doesn't refer to the kingdom as often as the Synoptic Gospels do, but on a few occasions, he refers to those excluded from the kingdom (1 Cor. 6:9–10; Gal. 5:19–21; Eph. 5:3–5). In each case there is a vice list specifying those who are disqualified from inheriting the kingdom. It isn't as if one will be excluded from the kingdom by definition if one has ever committed one of the sins named in these vice lists. After all, Paul acknowledges that the believers in Corinth came from such backgrounds and had indulged in such behaviors (1 Cor. 6:11). Because of the grace of God, believers are washed, sanctified, justified, and cleansed from all the sins they indulged in. Paul warns those who have new life in Christ that evil actions must not find a home in their lives. Or as it is framed in Galatians, those who continue to practice sinful behaviors are excluded from the kingdom (Gal. 5:21). The judgment is clearly retributive in that those excluded from the kingdom have indulged their selfish will and engaged in evil actions.

We see the same theme in Galatians 6:7–8, where the image of sowing and reaping is applied to the future world so that those who sow to the Spirit will reap eternal life but those who sow to the flesh will harvest "corruption" (*phthoran*). The contrast between eternal life and corruption clarifies that the final eschatological reward is in view, and the retributive principle is obvious since people reap what they sow. They harvest what they have planted. Interestingly, Travis says that the repayment isn't based on "the fruit of one's actions," claiming that recompense and retribution can't be in view because the punishment is "organic" and not "imposed from the outside."[19] The problem with this reading is that Travis splits apart what should be kept together. God truly punishes the wicked from the outside, but the punishment accords with what people do, and thus the punishment is organic and not arbitrary. Punishment is personal, organic, and retributive at the same time.

In 1 Corinthians 1:26–28, the judgment of the wise, strong, and elite will bring eschatological "shame" (*katischynē*) so that they are brought to nothing (*katargēsē*) and nullified on the last day. The judgment will reveal that those who disbelieve are proud of what they should be ashamed of, that they exult in what they should mourn over, that

---

19   Travis, *Christ and the Judgement of God*, 81.

they find pleasure in what should disgust them. They are set aside or nullified, not because God is vindictive and limited in his affections but because they have become ugly and dreadful—their humanity has been horribly defaced by evil. The same verb (*katargēsē*) is used in 1 Corinthians 15:24, which speaks of the last day when all demonic forces and spiritual powers will be set aside. The thought is the same as we saw previously. These cosmic forces can't live in a world of perfect beauty and goodness, their evil can't tolerate the bright light of goodness, and God can't allow such evil to live in a perfect world since it would disfigure it.

General Epistles

The General Epistles (including Hebrews in this case) refer to judgment in various ways. Although the profile of each letter could be sketched in, for our purposes, the letters will be studied together to gain a portrait of judgment. James designates God as the Judge, and the coming judgment is envisioned (James 5:9). Or as Hebrews says, the God of all people everywhere will judge the world (Heb. 12:23). This makes sense because rendering final judgment is what it means to be God, since all creatures are accountable to their Creator. The life of every human being is lived in his presence, and we will give an account to him on the final day. Our lives at times may seem routine and prosaic, but life only comes along once, and after death is the day of judgment (Heb. 9:27).

Final judgment reminds us that life is serious and not trivial, that the decisions we make in life are weighty, and that our choices in life have eternal consequences. Life must be lived in light of the eschaton. There are no second chances after Jesus's return, since the resurrection and "eternal judgment" follow death (Heb. 6:2). All people will on the last day "give account to him who is ready to judge the living and the dead" (1 Pet. 4:5). Human beings will stand before the Lord and will be responsible for their actions. The very thought of such an encounter reminds us that the final judgment is awesome and "fearful" (*phobera*, Heb. 10:27), which explains why Peter says believers must conduct themselves in "fear," since God "judges impartially according to each one's deeds" (1 Pet. 1:17). Such fear isn't meant to paralyze us but to galvanize us, to propel us to action. God judges according to the work of each one, so we are reminded afresh that the judgment is fair and retributive. None will be punished in a way that doesn't accord with their behavior and true character. Therefore, "the day of judgment" will bring the "destruction [*apōleias*] of the ungodly" as the world is burned with fire (2 Pet. 3:7). This is the great "day of the Lord" mentioned so often in the prophets. On that day "the heavens will pass away with a roar, and the heavenly bodies will be burned up and dissolved" (2 Pet. 3:10; cf. 2 Pet. 3:12).

The Judge, Jesus, "is standing at the door," and his "coming [*parousia*] . . . is at hand" (James 5:8–9). Thus, believers need to exercise patience and desist from complaining. They are to leave judgment to God instead of judging one another, since God as the one who gave the law is also the one who exercises judgment (James 4:12). Jude emphasizes that the ungodly will be judged and that those who turn grace into a pretext for sin will experience God's displeasure (Jude 4). In Jude 14–15, he quotes 1 Enoch 1:9, interpreting the coming of the Lord in 1 Enoch as the coming of Jesus. He stresses again that when Jesus comes, the ungodly will be judged. We might expect Jude to quote something extraordinary from 1 Enoch since it has many fascinating and unusual stories. Instead he quotes a text that is quite ordinary, one asserting that the Lord will come and judge those who have given themselves over to evil.

Other texts describe the effects of judgment or what will happen when the judgment arrives. The author of Hebrews writes a sermon (Heb. 13:22), and its primary purpose is to warn believers not to fall away. The five warning texts all have this same purpose (Heb. 2:1–4; 3:7–4:13; 5:11–6:12; 10:26–31; 12:25–29). Those who drift away and commit apostasy will not "escape" (*ekpheugō*, Heb. 2:3; 12:25) when God assesses all people everywhere. Along the same lines, those who don't continue to believe and obey, who harden their hearts, will not enter God's rest (Heb. 3:11, 18–19; 4:1, 3, 5, 10, 11). In the Old Testament, rest is used of the promised land that Israel entered under the leadership of Joshua, but Hebrews applies the term typologically and eschatologically to heavenly rest believers will experience after death. Conversely, the punishment of unbelievers is that they will not enter God's rest, and thus we have the idea that unbelievers will experience sorrow, stress, and strife in the world to come.

Those who produce "thorns and thistles," practicing evil, are unqualified (*adokimos*) at the final judgment (Heb. 6:8), and this term often refers to those who are unqualified on the last day. Thus, Paul needs to run the race to the end to avoid being "disqualified" (*adokimos*, 1 Cor. 9:27). Similarly, those in whom Jesus doesn't dwell are disqualified (*adokimoi*) from salvation (2 Cor. 13:5), as are those with a "debased mind" (*adokimon noun*, Rom. 1:28). Jannes and Jambres were "disqualified" (*adokimoi*) because they resisted the gospel (2 Tim. 3:8), and similarly those of the circumcision party in Titus were "unfit" (*adokimoi*) because of their evil actions (Titus 1:16). So, too, those who fall away, according to Hebrews, will experience eschatological disqualification. Those who renounce Christ are "near to being cursed" (*kataras engys,* Heb. 6:8). The word translated "near" (*engys*) in some translations doesn't mean that those who fall away are near to being cursed but will actually avoid it. No, the author means that they are near a curse temporally! The curse is coming, and they will not escape it if they abandon and forsake Jesus. This is why he closes the verse by saying that the "end" or outcome or result (*telos*) will be burning (Heb. 6:8).

The reference to fire accords with the last warning in Hebrews, where the author picks up the words from Deuteronomy (Deut. 4:24; 9:3) that "our God is a consuming fire" (Heb. 12:29). Similarly, the readers are warned, in what is certainly a text about the final judgment, that there is "a fury of fire" (*pyros zēlos*) that will "consume the adversaries" (Heb. 10:27). These texts on the future judgment aren't addressed to unbelievers but to believers—in order to encourage them to persevere and remain in the faith. Surely the language of judgment here is metaphorical, but the metaphor points to an agonizing and eschatological reality that the readers should avoid by all means.

In the same text, the readers are told that if they depart from Christ they will experience a "punishment" (*timōrias*) that is worse than that assessed under the Mosaic covenant (Heb. 10:28–29). The punishment under the Mosaic covenant was earthly and temporal, where malefactors were put to death, but the punishment in Hebrews is heavenly and eternal, and thus the author draws a typological connection between judgment under the old covenant and judgment under the new covenant. Under the new covenant, the punishment isn't physical death but eternal death, and thus the judgment is escalated from the old covenant to the new covenant. Hence, those who depart from the faith will experience God's "vengeance" (*ekdikēsis*), as he justly recompenses them for their faithlessness (Heb. 10:30). The "fearful" (*phoberon*) prospect of falling "into the hands of the living God" (Heb. 10:31) awaits them, for those who fail to persist in faith will be "destroyed" (*apōleian*, Heb. 10:39). The word *apōleian* used in Hebrews 10:39 often designates end-time destruction, and it is contrasted with the eschatological possession of the soul.

James speaks of the eschatological "humiliation" (*tapeinōsei*) of the rich (James 1:10) in a manner similar to Paul (1 Cor. 1:27). Some mistakenly think James doesn't describe the judgment of the rich but rather the passing away of their riches. But James describes the passing away (*pareleusetai*) of *the rich themselves* (James 1:10). The next verse confirms this reading since the text doesn't say that riches will wither but instead says that the *rich man* will disappear and wither (*maranthēsetai*, James 1:11). This reading fits with James 5:1, which speaks of the "miseries" (*talaipōriais*) that will come on the rich. James speaks of the ungodly rich, who have withheld the wages of the poor, ignoring their plight (James 5:4), while living sumptuously themselves (James 5:5). In the last days, however, their flesh will be consumed like fire (James 5:3), which describes the eschatological punishment of the ungodly. Peter envisions the final day as one when God visits those who oppose him (1 Pet. 2:12), and on that day the Lord's opposition to evil will become apparent (1 Pet. 3:12). The "outcome" (*telos*) for those who resist the gospel on that day will be dire (1 Pet. 4:17–18).

We find much shared in common between 2 Peter 2 and the letter of Jude. For our purposes we don't have to adjudicate the issue of sources, though I have argued elsewhere that 2 Peter probably used and depended on Jude.[20] In any case, both write against false teachers who were almost certainly libertines, who probably appealed to and distorted Paul's gospel of grace in support of their licentious message (see 2 Pet. 3:15–16). Peter's opponents anticipate people in our own world in their claim that there would be no last judgment, that the world would go on without a second coming of Christ (2 Pet. 3:4–7). No judgment will come, according to these deviant teachers, because God will not intervene in the world. In their estimation, life will march on as it always has, and thus people will not be held accountable for their behavior. Jude's emphasis on judgment suggests that the false teachers confronted in his letter may have shared the same perspective, assuring themselves that nothing bad would happen to them in the future. Peter promises, however, that they will face "swift destruction" (*tachinēn apōleian*, 2 Pet. 2:1), and as noted above, the word used for destruction is commonly used for eschatological judgment. In 2 Peter 2:3, we are again told that the "destruction" (*apōleia*) of these teachers is coming, and that their "condemnation" (*krima*) has been pronounced "from long ago." Jude also speaks of a judgment (*krima*) that has been prescripted (*progegrammenoi*) from "long ago" (Jude 4). As noted, both Jude and Peter remark that right teaching has been twisted in defense of sin (Jude 4; 2 Pet. 3:16), and in the Petrine reference the distortion will lead to "their own destruction" (*apōleian*). The destruction will come on "the day of judgment" (*hēmeran kriseōs,* 2 Pet. 2:9) when the wicked will be corrupted (2 Pet. 2:12; cf. Jude 10). In 2 Peter 3:7, it is described as "the day of judgment and destruction of the ungodly" (*hēmeran kriseōs kai apōleias tōn asebōn anthrōpōn*). Jude uses the verb (*apōlonto*) translated "perished" to describe those who died in Korah's rebellion (Jude 11). The judgment in Korah's case was temporal, but

---

20 See Thomas R. Schreiner, *1 & 2 Peter and Jude*, CSC, 2nd ed. (Nashville: Holman Reference, 2020), 499–503.

there is also a typological appropriation so that the earthly disaster striking Korah and his friends presages a greater and final destruction on the last day.

Both Jude and Peter certify the coming judgment by looking to the past. Jude recalls that the Lord "destroyed" (*apōlesen*) the wilderness generation that did not trust his promise to bring them into the land, bound the angels who did not stay within proper limits, and annihilated Sodom and Gomorrah for their egregious sins (Jude 5–7). Peter also uses three examples: (1) the angels who sinned (i.e., "the sons of God" in Gen. 6:1–4) and who are confined before the final judgment, (2) the cataclysm poured out on the world during the flood, and (3) the decimation of Sodom and Gomorrah (2 Pet. 2:4–6). These judgments occurred in history, but they point to and anticipate the final judgment, serving as additional examples of typological escalation where judgments in history forecast the final judgment. Jude's use of the word "destroyed" (*apōlesen*) with reference to Israel's experience in the wilderness, then, isn't merely a historical curiosity but is a prelude to the final destruction on the last day, as the connection between Jude 4 and 5 indicates, since the judgment predicted in Jude 4 is explicated in Jude 5–7.

Similarly, the judgment of the angels (Jude 6), where they are confined during the present era, looks forward to "the judgment of the great day" (*krisin megalēs hēmeras*), which is clearly the final judgment. Jude makes explicit in the case of Sodom and Gomorrah that the judgment in history anticipates the judgment to come (Jude 7). The judgment of the cities functions as an "example" (*deigma*), and it is not only an example but a profile of the "eternal fire" (*pyros aiōniou*) to come. Typological escalation emerges in the case of Sodom and Gomorrah, for the judgment in history points to a greater judgment—a judgment by fire that never ends.

Peter's perspective on angels who sinned accords with Jude, in that the angels are being confined until the "judgment" (*krisin*) of the day that is coming (2 Pet. 2:4). When it comes to the judgment of the flood, Peter doesn't look forward to a further judgment in 2 Peter 2:5, but in

2 Peter 3:6–7, the judgment of the flood is correlated with the judgment by fire that will come on the last day. When it comes to Sodom and Gomorrah, Peter follows Jude's pattern (2 Pet. 2:6), explicitly informing the readers that the judgment of those cities functions as "an example of what is going to happen to the ungodly." Peter and Jude could scarcely be clearer: judgment is coming, and readers should continue to trust and obey to avoid being excluded from God's gracious presence.

Conclusion

The New Testament Epistles often forecast the coming judgment. Paul teaches that the judgment is fair and equitable, affirming that the Lord will judge according to works—some will experience wrath and anguish, while others joy, glory, and peace. Or, as Paul puts it in 2 Thessalonians 1, God's judgment is just; unbelievers aren't treated unfairly or capriciously. They receive what they deserve. The judgment threatened is death—final and eternal separation from God. At the same time, judgment is described in terms of destruction, signifying the final ruin of those who don't believe or obey the gospel.

The General Epistles describe judgment in a variety of ways, including references to destruction, fire, misery, and anguish. None of these ways of talking about the judgment are new but fit with what we have seen elsewhere. Whatever the image, they often warn the readers about the judgment that is coming, showing that it is a central and constitutive part of their message. They often take historical examples of judgment (such as what happened at the flood or to Sodom and Gomorrah) and eschatologize them so that the judgments in history forecast and anticipate a greater and final judgment on the last day. Warnings about judgment don't display lack of love but are the very essence of love. The biblical writers are shouting: Danger! They are telling us to flee from the wrath to come, to find refuge in the loving arms of God in Jesus Christ.

Judgment in the Book of Revelation

> *Hallelujah!*
> *Salvation and glory and power belong to our God,*
>   *for his judgments are true and just;*
> *for he has judged the great prostitute*
>   *who corrupted the earth with her immorality,*
> *and has avenged on her the blood of his servants.*

REVELATION 19:1–2

Introduction

Some tend to think that Revelation is an outlier in the New Testament in emphasizing judgment, concluding that it reverts to the Old Testament vision of an angry God. We know from the previous chapters, however, that such a claim isn't true: judgment pervades and permeates the New Testament documents.[1] John often warns about the coming judgment in Revelation, but some of the judgments refer to

---

1 I should also mention that there is a minority report today where a few scholars claim that the message of Revelation is actually nonviolent, in that there will be no future judgment of the wicked. Some assert, then, that the book promises universal salvation for all. I have discussed this in my commentary on Revelation and will not spend time refuting that reading here. See Thomas R. Schreiner, *Revelation,* BECNT (Grand Rapids, MI: Baker Academic, 2023), 52–55.

punishments in history, not the final judgment. We see such historical judgments in the first four seal judgments (Rev. 6:1–8), the first
six trumpet judgments (8:6–9:19), and perhaps in some of the bowl
judgments (16:1–21). The judgments in history anticipate and point to
the final judgment, but they are not my concern here since the focus
in this work is on the final judgment.

A reference to the final judgment surfaces early in the book:
"Behold, he is coming with the clouds, and every eye will see him,
even those who pierced him, and all the tribes of the earth will wail
on account of him. Even so. Amen" (Rev. 1:7). John merges together
Daniel 7:14 and Zechariah 12:10. Daniel features the coming of the
son of man in the clouds to the Ancient of Days, and Zechariah
points to the grief that will fill the hearts of Israelites when they
gaze on the one they pierced. Here the coming isn't referring to
the Ancient of Days in the heavens but to the second coming of
Christ to the earth, a coming that is described further in Revelation
19:11–21. The context from which the citation hails in Zechariah
points to mournful repentance, and thus some interpreters think
John does not have judgment in mind but rather a coming that
produces salvation. This reading is possible, but I suggest it goes
astray for three reasons.

First, John often tweaks and adjusts Old Testament texts for his
own purposes. In Daniel 7, the son of man approaches the Ancient
of Days in the heavens, but in Revelation he comes to the earth. In
Zechariah, the Jews mourn over the one they pierced, but in Revelation 1:7, "all the tribes of the earth" (not just the Jews) mourn.
John probably draws on the larger message of Zechariah where
the prophet anticipates the day when "all the nations of the earth"
will congregate against the people of God (Zech. 12:3), and "all the
nations" that stand against Jerusalem will be destroyed (12:9). On
the last day, the Lord will fight against the nations (Zech. 14:3–4)
when he comes with "all the holy ones" (14:5). Thus, there are good
reasons to think that John drew a message of judgment from the
book of Zechariah itself.

Second, Matthew also brings together Daniel 7:14 and Zechariah 12:10 in his eschatological discourse (Matt. 24:30), and there the people will mourn at Jesus's return since judgment is at hand. John doesn't give us any indication that he appropriates these texts in a way that differs from Matthew.

Third, in Revelation the second coming of Jesus is regularly used to encourage believers to be ready, since judgment will fall on the ungodly on that day (e.g., Rev. 2:5, 16, 25; 3:3, 11; 16:15). The sixth seal in 6:12–17 describes the coming day of the Lord, the day of final judgment. John uses apocalyptic language to foreshadow the coming judgment. The entire world will be turned upside down, signaled by a massive earthquake, the blackening of the sun, a bloodred moon, and falling stars. The sky will unravel, and mountains and islands will be displaced. All unbelievers will shudder with fear and plead for the rocks and mountains to crush them to avoid facing the wrath of God and the wrath of the Lamb (Rev. 6:16–17). Even though the language is symbolic and apocalyptic, there is a real referent, pointing to the fearsome judgment to come.

Judgment Comes from God

Clearly, the judgment isn't merely cause and effect in a mechanical sense, as if we have an account of the misery human beings have wrought in our world. All the bad effects in the world cannot be traced to the actions of human beings.[2] Rather, the coming judgment represents the wrath of God and the Lamb. In other words, judgment stems from God himself as he pours out his anger on a world that has resisted his will. Leon Morris rightly says,

> The God of the New Testament does not sit back and let "natural" laws bring about the defeat of evil. He is actively opposed to evil in every shape and form. Where unpleasant consequences follow

---

2 This impersonal view of wrath is evident in the work by Anthony Tyrell Hanson, *The Wrath of the Lamb* (London: SPCK, 1957), 9, 81, 85, 110, 164, 178–79.

on evil-doing His hand is in it. In any case it is difficult to see what meaning can be attached to an "impersonal process" . . . in a universe where God is all-powerful and omnipresent.[3]

The wrath of God and the Lamb is an expression of divine justice and holiness, and thus wrath should not be explained as a fit of uncontrolled and unrighteous rage. God's wrath doesn't contradict his goodness but manifests it. Fear of what is coming provokes human beings to ask who can stand in the great day of the wrath of God and of the Lamb. We discover in Revelation 7 that only those who have washed their robes in the blood of the Lamb—only those who have confessed their sins and asked for forgiveness—will be spared (Rev. 7:13–14). Thus, the judgment to come isn't inevitable—God in his mercy offers forgiveness. Those who repent, those who turn to God for cleansing in the blood of Christ, will stand in the judgment.

We should also note that the sixth seal represents the answer to the prayer of the martyrs in Revelation 6:10 where they ask the Lord, who is "holy" (*hagios*) and "true" (*alēthinos*), when he will "judge" (*krineis*) and "avenge" (*ekdikeis*) their blood. The prayer voiced can't be dismissed as a bad attitude or as contrary to the spirit of Jesus. These saints, after all, are no longer alive and, thus, sin is a thing of the past. Indeed, the sixth seal is an *answer* to this very prayer, which is supported by the fact that the sixth seal follows immediately *after* the prayer of the martyrs, showing that God himself concurs with their cry for justice. We should also note that they ask God as the one who is "holy and true" to act on their behalf. God's holiness and goodness aren't called into question by the judgment. Quite the contrary. The beauty of his goodness is verified and substantiated by judging those who are evil. Finally, the words "judge" and "avenge" point to God's justice. The word "avenge" has connotations in English that should not be read into the text, as if God is filled with uncontrollable rage and inflicts on people a punishment far out of proportion with what is deserved. Actually,

3   Leon Morris, *The Biblical Doctrine of Judgment* (Grand Rapids, MI: Eerdmans, 1960), 70–71.

the words "judge" and "avenge" both point to the same reality—that the punishment God inflicts on the wicked is just and right, that God will act to make everything as it should be. Another support for this interpretation is Revelation 8:1–5, which functions as the introduction to the seven trumpet judgments. The narrative in these verses shows that the trumpet judgments constitute an answer to the prayers of the saints that waft up like incense to God's throne (Rev. 8:4; cf. Ps. 141:2). The prayers ascend to God, and the angel, as God's representative and delegate, hurls the fire of judgment onto the earth (Rev. 8:5).

The book of Revelation often describes the last judgment, and this is hardly surprising since it speaks of the culmination of history. Just as the sixth seal brings us to the end of history, so too the seventh trumpet transports us to the last day, the day of judgment and reward. God moves against the nations because they are enraged against him (Rev. 11:18), evoking Psalm 2:1 and the futile rage of the nations against Yahweh and his anointed one. Still, according to Revelation 11:18, the day has now arrived when the rage of the nations will be stilled, when their voice will be muted forever. Now God's wrath has come.

We should note that the punishment comes from God, since some interpreters try to make the case that God doesn't actually punish those who do evil in Revelation, that the judgment is simply a matter of what human beings do to themselves. There is some truth in this—since the actions of human beings warrant judgment, and in one sense we destroy ourselves—but it misses the fact that God has set up the world in such a way that evil destroys people. In other words, the cause-effect schema isn't impersonal but comes from God himself. The biblical text takes us a step further than this since it refers to God's wrath, emphasizing that the judgment originates with God. The last day is one where "the dead" will "be judged" and people will be rewarded, whether for good or ill, so that those who corrupted and destroyed (*diaphtheirontas*) the earth will themselves be destroyed (*diaphtherai*, Rev. 11:18). God's wrath is unleashed on the last day, but the justice of the judgment is reinforced. Human beings are recompensed for what they have done, and destruction is reserved for those who engaged in destruction themselves.

Some have complained that the God of Revelation is vindictive, pouring out unrestrained wrath in every direction in a fit of uncontrolled fury. Certainly God's wrath is featured in the book, although some have tried to argue (in a way that is spectacularly unsuccessful) that all the references to God's wrath are misinterpreted and that all the judgments come from the hands of humans or even from Satan. A reference to the impact of human beings or of the devil has some merit. After all, the dragon in Revelation subverts the good order of the world with his schemes and plans, and human beings spread evil far and wide. At the same time, we see repeatedly that judgment (including the final judgment) comes from the hand of God. The Lord in his wrath punishes his enemies, but at the same time John reminds us that the punishments are deserved. For instance, the trumpet judgments are designed to bring people to repentance (Rev. 9:20–21), and the searchlight shines in these verses on those who refused to turn to God. It is as if they could see a train wreck coming and still refused to get off the train tracks of judgment. God in his love forecasts what is coming, entreating human beings to come to him for forgiveness, respite, and rescue. It would be a mistake to conclude from Revelation 9:20–21 that John teaches that no one ever repents or that mercy is a mirage; his point is that many are unmovable—they don't and won't see the handwriting on the wall. God's judgment, therefore, is warranted since many stubbornly refuse to turn to him for forgiveness.

The God of Revelation isn't arbitrary or whimsical, throwing down thunderbolts without cause. All people are judged according to their works (Rev. 20:12–13; 22:12) and are recompensed for what they have done. The judgment, then, isn't capricious but accords with one's character and life. In Revelation 14:17–20, the judgment is painted as a great harvest, and there is the implication that those who practice evil are trampled in the winepress of God's wrath because their fruit is defective, because their lives have been ruined and defaced by evil. They are reaping what they have sown. We notice again the reference to God's wrath, certifying that the judgment stems from God himself. Furthermore, John doesn't blink from the agony reserved for those who have given themselves to evil. We are told that "the cowardly, the faithless, the detestable, . . . murderers, the sexually immoral, sorcerers, idolaters, and all liars" will experience "the second death"—the "lake that burns with fire" (Rev. 21:8). We must not miss the fact that those who practice evil are destined for the lake of fire—to a great and terrible punishment, since they have given themselves to evil and have failed to repent. The same melody is played in Revelation 22:15, where those outside the holy city, the new Jerusalem, are described as dogs, sorcerers, sexually loose, murderers, idolaters, and liars. Their refusal to turn away from their sins disqualifies them from entering the city of God. They have chosen which city to inhabit, and it is Babylon.

God's Judgment Is Just

Revelation 15 brings us into the throne room of God's temple before the horrible plagues (the bowls of Rev. 16) are poured out. The bowls aren't merely the consequence of human sin, although that is included. They represent God's judgment on sin since "with them the wrath of God is finished" (Rev. 15:1). Nor is there any suggestion that God's judgments are off-center. They are good and perfect because his "ways" are "just and true" (*dikaiai kai alēthinai,* Rev. 15:3). God is ever and always "holy" (*hosios,* Rev. 15:4). Thus, the bowl judgments represent God's "glory" and "power" (Rev. 15:8).

There is no need to rehearse all the bowl judgments in Revelation 16, particularly since the focus in this work is on the final judgment. Still, some of the bowls clearly include the final judgment. For instance, bowl six points to the "battle on the great day of God the Almighty" (Rev. 16:14), to the day, as Revelation 16:15 declares, when Jesus will return. Similarly, the seventh bowl (Rev. 16:17–21) announces the end of history with the declaration, "It is done!" (16:17). One has to wonder as these fearsome judgments descend on the earth if the judgments are excessive, more than people deserve. We might think that only modern people ask that question, but when we read the narrative carefully, we see that John was sensitive to that concern, and this sensitivity manifests itself at several points in Revelation 16.

For instance, what we find in Revelation 16:5–7 warrants a full citation:

I heard the angel in charge of the waters say,

> "Just are you, O Holy One, who is and who was,
>   for you brought these judgments.
> For they have shed the blood of saints and prophets,
>   and you have given them blood to drink.
> It is what they deserve!"

And I heard the altar saying,

> "Yes, Lord God the Almighty,
>   true and just are your judgments!"

Several features in these verses should be noted.

First, John pauses the bowl judgments to insert these parenthetical remarks. The intermission is striking because we don't find such a break in the first six seal or trumpet judgments, yet right in the midst of the bowl judgments John steps aside to speak to the readers. The structure of the text—the fact that John interrupts the narrative to insert these words—signals to us that these words are of great importance.

Second, God is described as the "Holy One" (*hosios*) and as "just" (*dikaios*), as the one who reigns over all of history (Rev. 16:5). The God who pours out these judgments is beautiful and righteous in his character; there is no moral imperfection or stain; he never does what is wrong or even what is partially wrong. John goes further: God's holiness and righteousness are manifested in his judgments. We should notice the causal conjunction "for" (*hoti*) in the verse. God is holy and righteous "for [because]" he "brought these judgments." As Richard Bauckham notes, the judgments "are not capricious one-off acts of a ruthless and unethical tyrant, but . . . demanded by the very nature of this righteous and holy God."[4] The judgments don't raise questions about his goodness but verify and uphold his rectitude.

Third, we have seen regularly that judgment is based on *lex talionis*—that is, the judgment is assessed according to the crime. In this case, the rivers and springs become blood (Rev. 16:4), and John says that those who practice evil are given blood to drink because they shed the blood of his people (Rev. 16:6). The punishment (drinking blood) fits the crime (shedding blood). Travis attempts to counter this reading by saying that we have a "poetic device,"[5] and this may be true, but the poetic expression has a clear retributive sense when we interpret it. Once again, the judgment isn't arbitrary or unfair. In fact, the angel who pronounces the words in Revelation 16:5–6 emphasizes this particularly by declaring that those who suffer punishment experience "what they deserve [*axioi*]" (16:6).[6]

Many today, reading about such severe plagues, would be quick to disagree and would assert that such punishments are unwarranted. But we should stop and consider for a moment where John and his critics would agree. Both John and people in our own world today would concur that punishments must be deserved to be just. The disagreement comes from whether the judgments are truly deserved, and many today think that no divine punishment is ever warranted. For those who believe, as I do, that we have a divine perspective on reality, God's

4 Richard Bauckham, "Judgment in the Book of Revelation," in *The Book of Revelation: Currents in British Research on the Apocalypse*, ed. G. V. Allen, I. Paul, and S. P. Woodman, WUNT 2/411 (Tübingen: Mohr Siebeck, 2015), 55–56.

5 Stephen H. Travis, *Christ and the Judgement of God: The Limits of Divine Retribution in New Testament Thought* (Peabody, MA: Hendrickson, 2009), 280.

6 Travis (*Christ and the Judgement of God*, 281) avers that people receive the consequences of their actions but there is no retribution. He defends this notion by saying that John depends on Wisdom of Solomon 11 in this chapter. It is quite uncertain that John draws on Wisdom here, and the bowl judgments of Revelation 16 constitute God's wrath that the angels pour out on the earth (Rev. 15:7). We are told in Revelation 16:1 that they are "the seven bowls of the wrath of God." Furthermore, we see in Revelation 16:5–7 that God has "brought these judgments," that he is the one who has "given" the wicked blood to drink, and that the bowls represent his "judgments." The attempt to separate the consequences of sin from God himself must be deemed unsuccessful.

judgment is warranted. After all, only God knows at the end of the day whether a judgment is truly deserved or not. The opinion of human beings, which is partial and limited, can hardly be the final court of appeal. We recognize intuitively that some crimes are greater than others. Thus, destroying a hive of honey bees isn't as serious as killing a human being. The gravest crime of all is rejecting and sinning against the Creator of all, the Lord of the universe, the one and only true God.

Fourth, Revelation 16:7 affirms what has already been said, but in this verse the altar (or an angel of the altar) speaks. The reaffirmation plays an important role, impressing on readers the truth of what is affirmed here. The affirmation comes to the forefront with the word "Yes." Three different titles are used for God: he is "Lord," "God," and "the Almighty," indicating the greatness of God, or we could say the "Godness" of the Lord. We have here another hint that only God sees the whole picture, the end from the beginning, and that the perspective of human beings is limited both by our creatureliness and also by our sin. The Lord of history rightly discerns and decides the destiny of all. The altar affirms that God's "judgments" (*kriseis*) are "true" (*alēthinai*) and "just" (*dikaiai*). The repetition assures readers of the rightness, validity, and goodness of the judgments.

Judgment Will Bring Praise

The judgment of Babylon, which represents Rome, comes to the forefront in Revelation 17–18 and the beginning of Revelation 19. The harlot Babylon in these chapters stands in contrast with the bride, the wife of the Lamb. The first verse of the section (Rev. 17:1) emphasizes the "judgment" (*krima*) destined for Babylon, the great prostitute and whore. Remarkably, the beast and ten kings end up playing a role in the judgment meted out to Babylon (Rev. 17:16–17). Instead of collaborating with the prostitute, they will at some point betray her and form an alliance against her. Their attack on the prostitute will prove to be her undoing and dissolution, and she will face the Old Testament penalty for a prostitute who is the daughter of a priest: burning with fire (Lev. 21:9). What is remarkable, however, is how evil implodes on itself with the result that so-called friends turn against one another. Revelation 17:17 pulls back the curtain, providing a divine perspective on the internecine squabbling. God is working out his will in the immolation of Babylon, fulfilling his purposes and designs, ensuring that evil will meet its appointed end.

Babylon is judged according to its sins and recompensed double for its transgressions (Rev. 18:5–6).[7] Elsewhere the punishment fits the crime, and thus the notion that we have double punishment is alien to what we have found thus far. It is unlikely that the expression here should be taken literally.[8] We should interpret what John says hyperbolically, meaning that Babylon is judged completely for its sins.[9] Psalm 79:12 asks the Lord to repay sevenfold, but the number is hardly literal, and the same is probably true in this case. The judgment of Babylon will come in an instant (Rev. 18:10, 17, 19), reminding readers that the judgment is unexpected, which is a theme found in the Jesus tradition (Matt. 24:36–51; 25:1–10) and in Paul's writings (1 Thess. 5:1–3). Thus, the fact that the final judgment hasn't arrived (cf. 2 Peter 3) must not be misinterpreted as if that day will never come. The Lord alerts his people in advance about the surprise that is coming.

One of the startling features of the judgment of Babylon is that God's people are summoned to rejoice over its downfall and final judgment (Rev. 18:20). Similarly, the multitude in heaven exclaim "Hallelujah!" at the fall of Babylon (Rev. 19:1). We find a similar expression in Revelation 19:3,

Hallelujah!
The smoke from her goes up forever and ever.

---

7   Travis (*Christ and the Judgement of God*, 282–83) sees retribution in the text but then backs away by saying that "the equivalence is more linguistic than real" (282). The retributive character of the text isn't washed away so easily.

8   Rightly David L. Mathewson, *Revelation: A Handbook on the Greek Text,* Baylor Handbook on the Greek New Testament (Waco: Baylor University Press, 2016), 242.

9   Robert Mounce, *The Book of Revelation,* NICNT (Grand Rapids, MI: Eerdmans 1977), 325; Stephen Smalley, *The Revelation to John: A Commentary on the Greek Text of the Apocalypse* (Downers Grove, IL: InterVarsity Press, 2005), 448.

The four living creatures and twenty-four elders join in by singing praise to God (Rev. 19:4), and the praise continues to resound (19:5–6). On first glance, it seems that something is drastically wrong, as believers and angels seem to be guilty of *Schadenfreude*, where we have joy over another's misfortune, and it may seem particularly out of place since the joy is over the eternal judgment of the wicked. For John, the joy isn't sinful or inappropriate since heavenly beings join in the praise, and they are free from twisted notions of vengeance. The scandal for such praise is lessened when we recognize the reason for the joy. The call to rejoice is explained as follows in Revelation 18:20: "for God has given judgment for you against her." The clear sense is that Babylon receives what she deserves so that the penalty she imposed on others comes back on her head. We read further in Revelation 18:24 that the judgment is justified because

> in [Babylon] was found the blood of prophets and of saints,
>> and of all who have been slain on earth.

Babylon was guilty of indiscriminate murder, with an appalling violation of human rights, and the day of reckoning had come. The rationale for God's judgment is also voiced in Revelation 19:2:

> for his judgments are true and just;
> for he has judged the great prostitute
>> who corrupted the earth with her immorality,
> and has avenged on her the blood of his servants.

Babylon ravaged the earth with its idolatry and lashed out murderously against the people of God, showing that idolatry is never a private affair but always impacts the public sphere. John assures his readers, therefore, that God's "judgments" (*kriseis*) are "true" (*alēthinai*) and "just" (*dikaiai*). We have noted previously that the rightness of God's judgments is defended, and the repetition is no accident. We need to know that the executed judgments are fitting and good and that they accord with justice.

Still, we wonder about all the joy, exultation, and praise that erupts when Babylon is judged. Isn't such a response contrary to the teaching of Jesus, who instructed us to love our enemies and to pray for God's mercy on those who hate us (Matt. 5:43–48)? In answering this question, we need to consider the framework of the story, observing the time period in which the righteous rejoice. The fall of Babylon represents the final judgment, the day when all evil and injustice is stricken from the world, the day when goodness blossoms and fills the earth. Thus, there is no contradiction of the command to love our enemies since that command relates to this life and to this world. As long as life on earth lasts, we are to pray for our enemies, asking our Father to give us love for them so that we are granted grace to do good for them, pleading especially for their salvation. The praise and gladness and worship in Revelation 18–19, however, doesn't pertain to this life. It describes what happens on the day of final judgment. Here we have gladness at the world's end. The joy, then, is like the joy experienced when the evil regime of the Nazis was defeated in 1945, or it can be compared to the exultation people expressed when many countries were freed from communist oppression in the late 1980s and early 1990s. Millions and millions were murdered, tortured, and oppressed by these evil powers. In fact, the evil perpetrated by Babylon is beyond our imagination, and if we truly understood the extent of evil practiced, we would all experience post-traumatic stress disorder. Babylon, which is not only Rome but also the city of man generally, represents the sum and substance of all human evil and oppression. The defeat of Babylon, therefore, brings joy because it signals the end of all human barbarism, brutality, and cruelty.

Once we understand this, the failure to rejoice would constitute a moral failure, as if we sympathized with a bloodthirsty regime, indifferent to the continued flourishing of a vicious power that crushes the helpless and impoverished beneath its feet. Peter Leithart reminds us that "we live in a world where ISIS warriors behead Christians and release the film, where Boko Haram kidnaps Christian girls as child-brides for Islamic husbands, where the church is being driven from her Middle Eastern birthplace."[10] During this life we recognize and hate injustice as well, but we pray for our enemies, longing for their repentance. When the final curtain comes down, when the eschaton arrives, the day for repentance is over. Then we rejoice over the downfall of evil and the judgment God imposes for the wickedness perpetrated. Morris captures the truth: "Judgment means that evil will be disposed authoritatively, decisively, finally. Judgment means that in the end God's will will be perfectly done."[11] The day of judgment is the day of kingdom come, the day when God's will shall be done.

Judgment Is Deserved

Some, of course, think that forgiveness should be extended by God even after death, that all crimes should be forgiven no matter what people have done, and that no one should ever be punished. We can understand such a sentiment and may even wish it were so. Such a state of affairs, however, trivializes life on earth, rendering null and void the lives we have lived. It ends up saying that our moral choices and our relationship to God on earth don't really matter, since God wipes the slate clean for all. I think many would agree that this latter perspective cancels the moral seriousness of our existence. Instead, the biblical worldview is that the choices and decisions made in this life have awesome significance. God renders to us according to what we have done. There is a moral calculus in the universe. To put it another way, God is the one who has infinite knowledge and wisdom. As the Judge of the entire earth, he does what is right (Gen. 18:25). We can trust that no one will be punished eternally who doesn't deserve it since his judgments are true and righteous, expressing his holy character.

The last judgment is portrayed in Revelation 19:11–21, where Jesus returns with majesty on a white horse and the armies of heaven follow him. The beast, the false prophet, and their troops are poised for the

---

10 Peter J. Leithart, *Revelation 12–22*, ITC (London: Bloomsbury T&T Clark, 2018), 267.
11 Morris, *The Biblical Doctrine of Judgment*, 72.

fight. The outcome of the fight is scarcely in question since the battle is against the King of kings and the Lord of lords (Rev. 19:16).

Some have argued that the last judgment isn't intended here, that what we see is the triumph of the gospel through the word of God. Such a reading is fascinating and attractive but almost certainly wrong. We see from the outset (Rev. 19:11) that Jesus comes to judge (*krinei*), and in every instance in Revelation this verb is used for judging God's enemies and never to designate his saving work (Rev. 6:10; 11:18; 16:5; 18:8, 20; 19:2; 20:12, 13). He also "makes war" (*polemei*) in Revelation 19:11. This same verb in Revelation 2:16 clearly denotes judgment, and, in any case, that is surely the natural meaning of the word. Similarly, Jesus's eyes "like a flame of fire" (Rev. 19:12) also denote judgment. This is verified by Revelation 2:18 where the eyes of Jesus are "like a flame of fire" (cf. also Rev. 1:14), and thus he sees what is happening in Thyatira with Jezebel and will judge accordingly. The judgment meted out isn't superficial but accords with the character of those judged since Jesus has infinite and comprehensive knowledge of all people.

Some think a "robe dipped in blood" (Rev. 19:13) refers to redemption, and the references to Jesus's atoning blood elsewhere in Revelation (1:5; 5:9; 7:14; 12:11) support this interpretation. But context is king, and in Revelation 19 the blood doesn't designate redemption but the blood of enemies that will be shed. This fits with the cry of the martyrs who ask the Lord to avenge their blood (Rev. 6:10; cf. 19:2). The final judgment is also portrayed as blood flowing "for 1,600 stadia [about 184 miles]" (Rev. 14:20). Most important for Revelation 19 is the Old Testament background, for the reference to blood hails from Isaiah 63 where Yahweh comes from Edom. Edom often stands in the Old Testament for the enemies of the Lord (see Isa. 34), for those who deserve his judgment. In Isaiah, the Lord's clothes are "red" and his "garments like his who treads in the winepress" (Isa. 63:2). Are his clothes red because he is saving? The answer is no and yes, but the no is more germane for our purposes than the yes. The whole portrait painted in Isaiah 63 is one of judgment. Yahweh tramples the winepress with furious anger, and the "lifeblood" of his adversaries "spattered on my garments" (Isa. 63:3). It is the day of God's "vengeance" (Isa. 63:4), where he is wrathful (63:5), where

> I trampled down the peoples in my anger;
>> I made them drunk in my wrath,
>> and I poured out their lifeblood on the earth. (Isa. 63:6)

But doesn't the context speak of salvation (Isa. 63:1, 5) and redemption (63:4) as well? Yes, but the redemption and salvation of Israel come when the Lord judges their enemies! The salvation of God's people and the judgment of enemies aren't antithetical but correlative. The Lord saves his people *by judging their enemies*, and without the judgment of Edom there would be no salvation for Israel. The Isaiah background confirms that the blood on Jesus's robe signifies judgment, just as it does in Isaiah 63.

The sword coming from Jesus's mouth (Rev. 19:15) could conceivably denote the efficacy of God's word to save. But the term "sword" is never used to designate God's saving word in Revelation. The "sharp two-edged sword" points to judgment (Rev. 1:16). For instance, in Pergamum some were holding onto the teaching of Balaam and the Nicolaitans, veering off into idolatrous practices. Jesus threatens to make war "with the sword of my mouth" (Rev. 2:16; cf. also 2:12). Clearly the sword is one of judgment, and the same is true in Revelation 19:15. In fact, the sword of Jesus's word is intended to "strike down [*pataxē*] the nations" (Rev. 19:15). The word "strike" (*patassō*) is never used for salvation but is often used to describe judgment of one kind or another, both in the Septuagint and the New Testament (cf. LXX Gen. 8:21; 19:11; Ex. 3:20; 9:15; 12:12; 32:35; Lev. 26:24; Num. 14:43; 33:4; Deut. 2:33; 28:22; Judg. 20:37; 1 Sam. 6:19; Pss. 3:8 [3:7 ET]; 135:10; Isa. 11:4; 19:22; 30:31; 60:10; Jer. 2:30; 40:5 [33:5 ET]; Hos. 6:1; Amos 3:15; Hag. 2:22; Zech. 12:4; Mal. 3:23 [4:6 ET]; Matt. 26:31; Acts 12:23; Rev. 11:6). The verb is often used as well for killing one's enemies, and thus there is no basis in the context of Revelation 19 for thinking that the striking of the nations is redemptive. Indeed, the rest of the text points in the opposite direction.

Judgment is also indicated by the clause, "He will rule [or "shepherd"; *poimanei*] them with a rod of iron [*rhabdō sidēra*]" (Rev. 19:15). Some take this to mean that Jesus shepherds the nations with authority, removing any notion of judgment. Such a reading in context is quite unlikely, especially since the next phrase refers to God's wrath (see below). Further support for this reading is the context of Psalm 2 from which this image is taken, for the iron rod in the psalm (Ps. 2:9) stands in parallel with the nations being shattered like pottery, which clearly refers to judgment. In addition, Psalm 2:9 is alluded to in Revelation 2:27, where we also find the notion of the shattering (*syntribetai*) of pottery, which substantiates a reference to judgment rather than salvation or loving shepherding. As noted, the next clause also points to judgment: "He will tread the winepress of the fury of the wrath of God the Almighty" (Rev. 19:15). Not much commentary is needed since it is quite clear that the wrath of God trampling his enemies points to judgment.

The scene shifts slightly in Revelation 19:17–21, but it is the same battle, and thus it is a mistake to bracket off Revelation 19:11–16 from the end of the chapter. Evoking the judgment of Gog and Magog (Ezek. 39:4, 17–20), birds are summoned for a grisly feast, and they consume the flesh of the armies opposed to the Christ. Every feature in the text supports a reference to the judgment because the text winds up with the beast and false prophet cast into the lake of fire (Rev. 19:20).

Since Revelation 19:11–21 is disputed, I have lingered over it to verify that judgment is truly taking place, and the evidence is compelling. We have a clear reference to the final judgment, to the day when the beast and false prophet will be removed once for all time. John is still concerned to impress on the reader the rightness and goodness of what is occurring, informing us that Jesus is "Faithful and True" (Rev. 19:11). In the same verse, he also assures the readers that "in righteousness" (*dikaiosynē*) Jesus "judges and makes war." The final judgment isn't a miscarriage of justice; it isn't the vengeful and arbitrary act typical of the Greek gods. God's judgment is measured and proportionate so that each person receives what is deserved.

Judgment Is Eternal

Revelation speaks of the final judgment as the lake of fire and sulfur. The phrase "lake of fire" is used five times in four verses (Rev. 19:20; 20:10, 14, 15). We are also told that the lake burns with sulfur (Rev. 19:20; 21:8; cf. 20:10). The images should not be taken literally, particularly in an apocalyptic book. Still, the referent points to agony and pain, and thus removing the literalness of the image doesn't lessen in the least the awfulness of the punishment. Only those who aren't in "the book of life" are cast in the lake of fire (Rev. 20:15), and thus this punishment is reserved only for the wicked. The lake of fire is also described as "the second death" (Rev. 20:14; 21:8). Those who conquer—that is, those who participate in "the first resurrection"—will be spared the second death (Rev. 2:11; 20:6). The phrase "second death" is apposite, for all people experience the first death, which is physical death. The second death is reserved for those who are separated from God, and it is particularly horrible.

It is also important to see that the final punishment in the lake of fire should be understood as eternal conscious punishment.[12] We read in Revelation 20:10, "The devil who had deceived them was thrown into the lake of fire and sulfur where the beast and the false prophet were, and they will be tormented day and night forever and ever." The final residence of the devil, the beast, and the false prophet is the lake of fire. The beast and false prophet may be corporate entities, but they are also likely represented by individuals, just as the beasts in Daniel 7 represent both kingdoms and kings. What stands out is that the torment will persist forever. John impresses on the reader the continual nature of the torment, saying it will continue "day and night" and then adds "forever and ever." Torment (*basanisthēsontai*) points to a conscious existence, one where those suffering are cognizant of their punishment. To put it another way, torment doesn't fit with annihilationism, particularly torment that lasts forever since

---

12 Such a theme was also common in Jewish literature: 4 Macc. 13.14–15; 2 Esd. 7.36–38; 4 Ezra 7.36–38; 2 En. 10.1–3; T. Isaac 5.21–32; Sib. Or. 2.203–5.

the very point of annihilationism is that the consciousness of those punished is obliterated.

The most important text regarding the nature of future punishment is Revelation 14:9–11. It is important enough to warrant quoting it in full:

> And another angel, a third, followed them, saying with a loud voice, "If anyone worships the beast and its image and receives a mark on his forehead or on his hand, he also will drink the wine of God's wrath, poured full strength into the cup of his anger, and he will be tormented with fire and sulfur in the presence of the holy angels and in the presence of the Lamb. And the smoke of their torment goes up forever and ever, and they have no rest, day or night, these worshipers of the beast and its image, and whoever receives the mark of its name."

Those who give themselves to the influence of the beast will experience the full fury of God's wrath in the "cup of his anger" (Rev. 14:10). We find the same verb used with reference to the devil, the beast, and the false prophet in Revelation 20:10. Those who succumb to the beast's influence "will be tormented [*basanisthēsetai*] with fire and sulfur" (Rev. 14:10), and there is no indication that the torment will be limited in time.[13] The verb "torment" points to conscious punishment. Indeed, the punishment will occur in the presence of the angels and the Lamb. It is difficult to know why this detail is added; perhaps it is to emphasize that they have cut themselves off from the source of life. Augustine, speaking of the eternal punishment of the devil, says,

> Why has the church been so intolerant with those who defend the view that, however greatly and however long the devil is to be punished, he can be promised ultimately that all will be purged or pardoned? Certainly it is not because so many of the church's saints

---

13 See Pierre Prigent, *Commentary on the Apocalypse of St. John*, trans. Wendy Pradels (Tübingen: Mohr Siebeck, 2001), 444; Greg Beale, *The Book of Revelation*, NIGTC (Grand Rapids, MI: Eerdmans, 1999), 761–63; Craig R. Koester, *Revelation: A New Translation with Introduction and Commentary*, Anchor Bible (New Haven, CT: Yale University Press, 2014), 614.

and biblical scholars have begrudged the devil and his angels a final cleansing and the beatitude of the kingdom of heaven. Nor is it because of any lack of feeling for so many and such high angels that must suffer such great and enduring pain. This is not a matter of feeling but of fact. The fact is there is no way of waiving or weakening the words the Lord has told us.

He remarks, "These are words that have a single meaning in the divine Scripture, namely, of unending duration."[14]

John then tells us that "the smoke of their torment" will ascend forever (Rev. 14:11). The noun "torment" (*basanismou*) comes from the same root as the verbal form. Some claim that the smoke ascends forever but not the torment.[15] Such a reading is improbable since it seems most natural to say that the smoke rises forever because the suffering continues unabated.[16] The rest of Revelation 14:11 confirms this interpretation. Those who give themselves to the beast and take its mark will not find "rest, day or night." One could say, of course, that they don't find rest because they are blotted out of existence, but the words "day or night" suggest ongoing existence, just as we saw in Revelation 20:10. Furthermore, the claim that they find no rest suggests that they are seeking relief and respite, just as the rich man seeks relief from his torment by asking Abraham to send Lazarus with a drop of water for his tongue (Luke 16:23–24).

---

14 Cited in W. C. Weinrich, ed. and trans., *Revelation*, ACCS: New Testament, vol. 12 (Downers Grove, IL: InterVarsity Press, 2005), 342. Weinrich cites Augustine's *City of God* 20.14; 21.3 (Fathers of the Church: A New Translation [Washington D.C.: Catholic University of America Press, 1947).

15 Cf. G. B. Caird, *A Commentary on the Revelation of St. John the Divine* (New York: Harper & Row, 1966), 166–67; Clark H. Pinnock and Robert C. Brow, *Unbounded Love: A Good News Theology for the Twenty-First Century* (Downers Grove, IL: InterVarsity Press, 1994), 91–94; Philip Edgecumbe Hughes, *The True Image: The Origin and Destiny of Man in Christ* (Grand Rapids, MI: Eerdmans, 1989), 398–407; Smalley, *The Revelation to John*, 367–68. See the larger defense for annihilationism in Edward Fudge, *The Fire That Consumes: A Biblical and Historical Study of the Doctrine of Final Punishment*, 3rd ed. (Eugene, OR: Cascade, 2011).

16 So Leithart, *Revelation 12–22*, 354.

We have seen repeatedly in Revelation that the judgments levied by the Lord are righteous and good and just. It is clear that this includes eternal conscious punishment. Many naturally flinch at such a conclusion, and some, perhaps many, also protest that such unending judgment can't be right. But the first thing that needs to be asked is this: How do we know that? How can we be so sure that our sense of what is fitting and right in judgment is correct? If we claim that eternal conscious punishment is unjust, we are claiming to have a God's-eye view of what is just and right. We are claiming to see clearly enough to pass judgment on judgment, declaring that we know what is right and just and fitting. Finite human beings don't and can't know enough to say such, and the better stance—the humble stance, the creaturely stance—is to say that the Judge of all the earth knows and does what is right (Gen. 18:25). We must remember that his judgments are unsearchable and his ways inscrutable (Rom. 11:33) and that the Lord doesn't need our counsel or advice (Rom. 11:34).

We also have to beware of exalting love over holiness, as if the former is more important than the latter. Our society, the time in which we live, often doesn't think eternal judgment is warranted because we think lightly of human sin. Sin seems excusable and always forgivable. We need to remember that forgiveness is offered to all, but not all receive the offer. Many reject the light shining in the darkness, and such a choice has consequences. Life isn't merely sound and fury signifying nothing. Instead, what we make of our lives has eternal significance. The permanent punishment of sin displays the beauty and necessity of absolute holiness and purity and goodness. Sin against God, as many theologians have said, has infinite consequences because he is infinitely perfect and beautiful. As creatures, our task isn't to answer every question but to trust the wisdom and the word of the one who is "high and lifted up," whose "name is Holy" (Isa. 57:15). Many might say that failing to answer every question represents a sacrifice of the intellect. But recognizing the limits of our intellect is humble. As creatures, we can't answer every question, and this is hardly surprising. We expect that the thoughts of the Creator would transcend our thoughts, that his wisdom and knowledge would far surpass ours.

Conclusion

The book of Revelation brings us to the end of history, so it is not surprising that it often addresses the matter of final judgment. The judgment is painted in apocalyptic colors and images, and we should not confuse the images with the referent. Still, we could make the mistake of concluding that the judgment isn't real or that it isn't terrifying. Even if the judgment is portrayed symbolically, it is no less real and frightening. King Jesus will have the last word. The wicked—whether Satan, the beast, the false prophet, or Babylon—will not triumph. Evil is on the wrong side of history, and God will pull it down from its heights and remove it forever. The saints who have been discriminated against, mocked, persecuted, and killed will be vindicated. God's kingdom will come, and his will shall be done. A new day is coming, a new heaven and earth will dawn, and all those who enjoy and practice evil will be excluded from the heavenly city. The sorrows, tears, futility, and heartache of the present age will be over. And we will see more clearly than we do now that God's judgment of the wicked is just. We will rejoice over the judgments of God. We will praise him that evil has been dethroned. Every question about the rightness of God's judgments will be stilled, and we will see that the Lord is right and does what is right. Our hearts and minds will be at rest, and we will rejoice evermore.

Living in Light of the Judgment

For we must all appear before the judgment seat of Christ,
so that each one may receive what is due for what he
has done in the body, whether good or evil. Therefore,
knowing the fear of the Lord, we persuade others.

2 CORINTHIANS 5:10–11

Introduction

The coming judgment isn't an abstract reality describing a future day that is disconnected from our everyday lives. In the narrative of Scripture, the final judgment addresses the lives of both believers and unbelievers, and in this chapter we will consider what the final judgment says about our daily lives. Four themes will be considered: (1) the call to godliness, (2) the admonition to persevere in faith, (3) the promise of deliverance from the wicked, and (4) the summons to repentance.

Call to Godliness

The final judgment reminds us that we are to fear the Lord, and such fear leads to godliness. Jesus warned his disciples that the one true God could do something far worse than killing them physically; he could hurl them into hell (Luke 12:5). The fear of the Lord should not be understood as a paralyzing fear that utterly disables us. Fear of the Lord should galvanize us to action, to giving ourselves entirely to God, to a life devoted to him.[1] Even though we are not to be immobilized by fear, there is a healthy dread of the Lord, a recognition of his flaming holiness. When Uzzah was struck down for touching the ark (2 Sam. 6:6–7), David "was afraid of the LORD" and wondered how he could survive in God's presence (2 Sam. 6:9). Or we think of the story where the Lord sent lions to maul and kill those who didn't fear the Lord (2 Kings 17:25), revealing that he is to be revered as the great and awesome God. As the psalmist declares, he is

> a God greatly to be feared in the council of the holy ones,
>   and awesome above all who are around him. (Ps. 89:7)

The fear of God is closely tied to the judgment, to standing before him on the last day. This is reflected in Psalm 90:11,

> Who considers the power of your anger,
>   and your wrath according to the fear of you?

Those who know the one true God "fear" his "judgments" (Ps. 119:120); such fear isn't the mark of spiritual immaturity, as if we ever outgrow such a fear. As Isaiah the prophet says, "But the LORD of hosts, him you shall honor as holy. Let him be your fear, and let him be your dread" (Isa. 8:13). The fear of the Lord isn't paralyzing, but there is fear—a kind of dread or terror—that motivates us to turn to God, even if this isn't the only or even primary motivation.

It is remarkable how often in the Scriptures that the fear of the Lord is tied to living righteously, to living in a way that pleases God. Deuteronomy regularly connects fearing the Lord with the observance of his commands (Deut. 5:29; 6:2, 24; 8:6; 13:4; 17:19; 31:12; see also 1 Sam.

---

1   On the fear of the Lord, see Michael Reeves, *Rejoice and Tremble: The Surprising Good News of the Fear of the Lord* (Wheaton, IL: Crossway, 2021).

12:14; 2 Chron. 6:31; Job 1:1, 8; Ps. 34:11–14; Eccl. 12:13; Eph. 5:21; 6:5; Phil. 2:12). The fear of the Lord should not be restricted to keeping the Lord's commands externally, for those who truly fear the Lord obey from the heart. This is summed up well in Deuteronomy 10:12: "And now, Israel, what does the LORD your God require of you, but to fear the LORD your God, to walk in all his ways, to love him, to serve the LORD your God with all your heart and with all your soul?" Fearing God, loving him, and worshiping him are inextricably intertwined, and such fear involves the entire person, as we give all we are to the Lord. Those who fear the Lord don't worship other gods (2 Kings 17:35, 37, 38), and they place their trust and hope in God (Ps. 115:11). When people fear the Lord, their hearts are inclined toward him so that they don't depart from following him (Jer. 32:40). True wisdom consists of fearing the Lord (Job 28:28; Ps. 111:10; Prov. 1:7; 9:10), and wisdom manifests itself in living wisely and righteously so that we don't prize our own discernment over the revelation of the Lord (Prov. 3:7). God's word of instruction, his torah, guides our lives, which means that those who fear the Lord hate and turn away from evil (Prov. 8:13; 16:6).

Fearing God makes a difference in our everyday lives. The Amalekites, by killing Israelite stragglers as they made their way to the land of promise, revealed that they didn't fear God (Deut. 25:18), but the prophet Obadiah showed his fear of God in rescuing prophets from the hands of the murderous Jezebel (1 Kings 18:12–13). Similarly, the midwives who feared the Lord responded by not murdering babies, contrary to the orders of Pharaoh (Ex. 1:17), and those who fear the Lord keep their promises even if doing so brings adversity (Ps. 15:4). The connection between fearing God and doing what is right is evident in that those who fear God treat the deaf, the blind, and the elderly with kindness, compassion, and respect (Lev. 19:14, 32). We see that Nehemiah feared God because he didn't oppress the people when he served as governor and didn't take advantage of them financially (Neh. 5:15). Fearing the Lord isn't an abstraction but changes how we live in the concrete realities of everyday life, as we live every moment in his presence.

Admonition to Persevere in Faith

Most people naturally connect the final judgment, the threat of hell, with a call for unbelievers to repent, and they are not wrong to do so, as we shall see below. What is often missed, however, is the role that the judgment plays in the lives of believers. The threat of judgment doesn't apply solely to unbelievers but addresses believers as well. We see in several texts that believers are encouraged to persevere in the faith in light of the judgment to come.

The call to persevere informs 2 Thessalonians 1:5–10, a text discussed above in terms of final judgment. The future revelation of Jesus from heaven with the angels is predicted. On that day he will flame forth in justice against those who disobey and have no knowledge of God. Eternal separation from God's gracious presence and his saving power will be the destiny of unbelievers. On the other hand, believers will see the beauty of Christ and marvel with astonishment. If we pause to think about who was reading what Paul wrote about the future judgment and the fate of unbelievers, we realize that these verses weren't written to unbelievers but to believers. Paul writes to *believers* about the fate of unbelievers. Why does he do that? Certainly not to rejoice over the destiny of those who will suffer punishment in the future.

When we look at the context of the chapter, Paul's main reason for bringing up the final judgment surfaces. God is thanked for the faith and love of the Thessalonians, even though they were suffering from persecution (2 Thess. 1:3–4). The believers were being mistreated and victimized by their contemporaries (2 Thess. 1:6–7), and their life in society was difficult because of their newfound faith. The chapter ends with a prayer that the saints in Thessalonica will live in a way that is worthy of their calling (2 Thess. 1:11–12). Now we are in a position to understand why the believers in Thessalonica were informed about the destiny of the ungodly. In the midst of their suffering and pain, they doubtless asked themselves if the Christian life was worth it. As they observed the lives of unbelieving neighbors, they saw that they were living relatively comfortable and hassle-free lives. Paul longed for these new believers to persevere in the faith, a theme that is prominent in the first letter to the Thessalonians as well (1 Thess. 3:1–10). Their endurance in the faith, their persistence amid adversity, makes a difference because those who don't belong to God will face adversity in the future, eternal adversity. Believers must not turn away from Jesus if they want to avoid the vengeance and suffering that will come upon the wicked.[2]

Paul brings up the reality of hell not to threaten and frighten unbelievers but to remind believers that their suffering has purpose and meaning, that enduring to the end makes an eternal difference. One motive (not the only motive!) for perseverance is avoiding the punishment to come. Paul doesn't think this is a substandard and spiritually immature reason to persevere. Of course, believers aren't only reminded of future punishment but are also given a picture of the indescribable joy and beauty awaiting them (2 Thess. 1:10). When Jesus appears, they will see a beauty that outranks any they have ever witnessed. They will see a glory that will make the loveliest flower pale in comparison.

First Peter 4:5 also forecasts the final day, when all "will give account to him who is ready to judge the living and the dead." Once again, the prospect of future judgment becomes a spur to perseverance. Peter reminds his readers about the Gentiles (i.e., unbelievers) who had given themselves over to evil lusts, drunken parties and orgies, and worship of false gods (1 Pet. 4:3). Those who are separated from Christ were astonished that believers didn't participate with them in such evil behavior, so they heaped abuse on the believers (1 Pet. 4:4). We need to remind ourselves that Peter doesn't write these verses to unbelievers; they weren't reading this letter! Peter writes to *believers about unbelievers*, and he doesn't do so to vilify unbelievers or to rejoice in the fact that they will be judged. He writes for the sake of believers. The purpose of 1 Peter 4:1–6 is to encourage believers to make a break with

2   I don't believe these warnings suggest that true believers can finally apostatize. Warnings are the *means* God uses to preserve the elect. For this theme see Thomas R. Schreiner, *Run to Win the Prize: Perseverance in the New Testament* (Wheaton, IL: Crossway, 2010); Thomas R. Schreiner and Ardel B. Caneday, *The Race Set Before Us: A Biblical Theology of Perseverance and Assurance* (Downers Grove, IL: InterVarsity Press, 2001).

sin—to be willing to suffer for Jesus's sake in the midst of a society that resists and abuses them. They are to commit themselves to God and pledge to live for his sake, for his glory, for the honor of his name. Thus, Peter features the judgment of the wicked to say to the godly: Don't go down their pathway; don't join with them in unbelief and godlessness. Unbelievers may ridicule and revile believers during the present era, but the day of judgment is coming. Perseverance in the faith is not an idle matter. If believers renounce their faith and cast their lot with unbelievers, they will face the judgment to come. They will suffer far more in the future if they apostatize than they suffer as believers in the present age. Peter reminds his readers of the judgment to prod them to endure, to remind them that siding with Christ makes a difference and that turning back to evil has eternal consequences.

In the previous chapter, we considered Revelation 14:9–11, which is surely one of the most frightening texts in the New Testament—even in the entire Bible. We read that those who adore and worship the beast and its image will experience God's unmitigated wrath. They will be tormented forever and will never find rest. Once again, this text wasn't written to terrorize unbelievers. It was written to the believers in the seven churches of Asia Minor. John directs them to contemplate the destiny of those who compromise, who make the emperor and his kingdom their god. He doesn't write about the destiny of unbelievers with a spirit of vengeance so that Christians will exult over the punishment of their enemies. Instead, he writes for pastoral reasons—to exhort and encourage his readers. Notice John's very next words after his vivid description of final punishment for those who worship the beast and his image: "Here is a call for the endurance of the saints, those who keep the commandments of God and their faith in Jesus" (Rev. 14:12).

The believers in the seven churches were suffering, and some were even being put to death (cf. Rev. 2:13; 6:9–11; 16:6; 17:6; 18:24; 19:2; 20:4). The temptation to avoid suffering was intense, and they could find relief if they compromised with the empire, succumbing to the blandishments of the society in which they lived. One motivation to endure—surely not the only reason—is to avoid the torment unbelievers will face. Believers are enjoined to consider the eschaton, to reflect on what will happen if they lapse. Such a state of affairs should launch them into a fresh commitment and desire to keep trusting in Jesus and to put into practice what God has commanded. Believers need to know that enduring suffering is worth it and that their continued trust during adversity will make an eternal difference.

Promise of Deliverance

The final judgment also means that the righteous are delivered from those who oppress them; they are rescued from their persecutors. The truth is captured well in Isaiah 35:4,

> Say to those who have an anxious heart,
>   "Be strong; fear not!
> Behold, your God
>   will come with vengeance,
> with the recompense of God.
>   He will come and save you."

Israel in this instance faces oppression and subjugation from enemies. The Lord promises that he will intervene and save his people, but he does so by inflicting vengeance and retribution on their enemies. Israel's salvation is coincident with the destruction of their adversaries. This is not a new story, since Israel's redemption and liberation from Egypt took place as the Egyptians were judged with devastating plagues. Relief and respite for Israel came as Egypt was removed as an oppressor.

This theme is tucked into several texts that we examined relative to the final judgment. For instance, when Jesus returns, the beast and the false prophet along with their armies will be defeated (Rev. 19:11–21). Similarly, at the end of history Babylon will meet its end, never to rise again (Rev. 17:1–19:5). At the end of the one thousand years, Satan will be cast into the lake of fire forever (Rev. 20:7–10). We see in Revelation enemies of believers who persecute the saints, discriminating against them financially, pressuring them socially, and depriving them of life physically. The relief that comes when oppressors cease to exert their influence in the world is almost palpable. The final judgment means that a new day is coming, a new world is coming, a world in which grief, pain, and tears are over (Rev. 21:4), a world in which everything is new (Rev. 21:5), where nothing evil can enter the holy city (Rev. 21:8, 27). The "great tribulation" in this life (Rev. 7:14) will be over, the Lamb will shepherd his people (Rev. 7:17), and the God who reigns on the throne will shelter them (Rev. 7:15).

We see the theme of relief as well in James 5. The chapter opens (James 5:1–6) with a portrait of the unbelieving rich who oppress their workers and hold back their pay. The rich live sumptuously and lavishly while discriminating against the righteous, even depriving them of their lives. James reminds his readers, however, that a day is coming when the rich who oppress the poor will experience misery and their wealth will be a distant memory. The day of vindication and respite for believers is coming, and thus they should be patient as the Lord's return is near (James 5:7–8). In the midst of their suffering it would be easy to complain and turn against one another, as stress and deprivation put everyone's nerves on edge (James 5:9). Believers are called to persevere and to endure suffering because the day when the Lord will shower mercy on his own is coming (James 5:10–11). This fits with Psalm 76:9 as well, which shows God's judgment of the wicked. When the day of judgment arrives, God will "save all the humble of the earth." Judgment removes the wicked from the scene, delivering the righteous from their hands. As I write these words, we see an illustration from contemporary life that is somewhat analogous. Russia, without provocation, has invaded Ukraine, killing, slaughtering, and raping many Ukrainians. Judgment day means the end of all oppressors and the vindication of those who belong to the Lord.

There is no need to linger on 2 Thessalonians again since the text has been brought up twice, but we should flag that the day of affliction for believers is the present evil age, the day when unbelievers are persecuting and troubling them (2 Thess. 1:6–7). Still, the day of punishment for those who don't know God and who don't obey the gospel is the day of "relief" (*anesin*) for believers (2 Thess. 1:7), the day when all their trials will end, the day when eternal joy begins. God will vindicate his own, showing that there is a moral calculus in the universe, that good and evil aren't illusions, that what we do in life truly makes a difference—an eternal difference.

I have mentioned earlier that we need to be careful about drawing too much from the parable of the rich man and Lazarus about the afterlife (Luke 16:19–31). The converse is true as well. It is also a mistake to say that nothing can be learned about our future destiny from the parable. Certainly the parable teaches that the good will be rewarded and that those who practice evil will be punished. Furthermore, it fits with what we have seen elsewhere to say that those who do evil will suffer anguish, although we must be careful about being too definite about the nature of their suffering. Similarly, it is legitimate to conclude that the future life for the redeemed will be one of comfort (*parakaleitai*, Luke 16:25). We are not privy to the details of that comfort. Still, the days of oppression, hunger, and mistreatment will have ended, and joy, consolation, and relief will be a reality forever for those who belong to God.

Summons to Repentance

I have been making the argument that the punishment of the wicked speaks to the lives of believers, reminding them to live in a way that pleases God, to persevere in the faith, and to look forward to the relief and consolation that is most certainly coming. At the same time, however, the judgment also constitutes a call for unbelievers to turn from their sin, to repent, and to put their faith in Christ. For instance, in Romans 2:1–5 Paul argues that God judges fairly and impartially, which means that those who harden their hearts and fail to repent will face God's righteous judgment. Still, the judgment isn't immediate, and God extends his kindness in not punishing immediately. The delay doesn't signify that there won't be a judgment but instead illustrates the love of God. He grants people time because he doesn't want any to perish but all to come to repentance (1 Tim. 2:4). We saw several times in the book of Revelation that God's judgments in history, the judgments forecasting the final judgment, are a call to repent (Rev. 9:20–21; 16:9, 11). The threat of judgment warns people of the cataclysm that is coming, of the day when there are no more opportunities to change one's mind. God's heart in declaring the judgment to come is captured in the unforgettable words of Ezekiel 18:32: "For I have no pleasure in the death of anyone, declares the Lord GOD; so turn, and live." God's desire for people to repent impresses upon us the truth that his judgments aren't whimsical or capricious.[3]

We find a similar theme in 2 Peter 3. The scoffers rejected the notion that Jesus would come again. Thus, they mocked the idea of a final judgment in which they were assessed for their actions. Peter assures his readers that a day of destruction is coming. Still, the question arises about why there is a delay, why Jesus has not yet returned. Peter gives more than one answer, but the one that concerns us is found in 2 Peter 3:9: "The Lord is not slow to fulfill his promise as some count slowness, but is patient toward you, not wishing that any should perish but that all should reach repentance." The Lord hasn't delayed his promise but is giving space and time for people to repent. He desires all to come to him for salvation. The ideology and worldview of the scoffers seems attractive since it absolves people of a future judgment, but it represents a world without any moral reckoning, a world where people do whatever they wish without any consequences for their actions and behavior. Such a world isn't paradise but a nightmare, where evil runs rampant forever. At the same time, those who doubt the final judgment are profoundly unloving, for they promise those who don't repent that there will be no consequences for their actions—when the opposite is the case. They don't warn others that they must turn to God before it is too late, which is remarkably cruel if a disaster is in the offing. We see again that God, because of his great love, provides an opportunity for those who have hardened their hearts against him. God informs us in advance about the judgment, and he isn't joking (cf. Gen. 19:14).

3   R. V. G. Tasker, *The Biblical Doctrine of the Wrath of God* (London: Tyndale Press, 1951), 15.

We are told about the judgment so that we will turn from our sins, put our faith in Jesus Christ, and escape the wrath to come.

Conclusion

We have seen in this chapter that the final judgment plays a role in the lives of both believers and unbelievers. The approaching day summons Christians to live godly lives, to give themselves to that which is good and right and true. At the same time, the judgment to come provokes believers to persevere. When Christians are suffering, the temptation arises to compromise, to surrender the faith, to return to one's former life. The desire for relief from pain and opposition may feel overwhelming. Still, believers are reminded that endurance makes a difference, that perseverance is a matter of life and death. If believers turn away from Christ, they will join the ungodly and face final judgment, which will inflict a pain far greater than anything they are experiencing now.

This leads to the third theme in the chapter, which is closely related to the previous one. On the day of judgment, believers will be delivered from all pain, tears, and sorrow. For believers, the day of judgment is a day of joy, a day when they will marvel over the beauty of Christ and a day when all their trials, sorrows, and sufferings cease. The final judgment also represents a call to unbelievers to repent and to turn to Christ for salvation. God in his kindness is patient, warning those who are separated from God about the wrath to come. God desires all to be saved, and thus all are invited to escape the terror that is coming. Judgment doesn't come without warning people of the danger that is looming, with the hope that those who hear the message will turn in faith to the one true God in Jesus Christ.

Salvation Shines Brighter

But you are a chosen race, a royal priesthood, a holy nation, a people for his own possession, that you may proclaim the excellencies of him who called you out of darkness into his marvelous light. Once you were not a people, but now you are God's people; once you had not received mercy, but now you have received mercy.

1 PETER 2:9–10

Introduction

When we truly see the holiness of God and understand that we deserve judgment, then we realize that we are in the same position as Isaiah: "Woe is me! For I am lost; for I am a man of unclean lips, and I dwell in the midst of a people of unclean lips; for my eyes have seen the King, the LORD of hosts" (Isa. 6:5). As Christians, we don't think of the judgment and look condescendingly on those who will be judged. If we see ourselves truly, we lament and grieve over our sin. We are deeply conscious of our own failings, our own rebellion, our own stubbornness, our own evil. Thus, we resonate with a question that permeates the biblical witness. We encounter it in 1 Samuel 6, when the ark was returned by the Philistines to Beth-shemesh. After the restoration of the ark, the people rejoiced with burnt offerings and sacrifices. But the day of rejoicing turned into one of mourning because some looked inside the ark, contrary to what God directed, and seventy people were struck dead (1 Sam. 6:19). We find in Leviticus 16 that only the high priest could enter the room where the ark of God's presence resided—and only once a year when he followed the detailed protocols. Thus, looking into the ark blatantly transgressed what the Lord had revealed to Israel. After committing this sin and being struck down, the survivors asked the question, "Who is able to stand before the Lord, this holy God?" (1 Sam. 6:20). That is the question for all of us when we consider the intensity and beauty of God's holiness.

The Judgment of God

We saw earlier that Psalm 76 is a key passage for our topic in that it features God's judgment. The question that surfaces is how anyone anywhere avoids God's judgment:

> But you, you are to be feared!
>> Who can stand before you
>> when once your anger is roused? (Ps. 76:7)

Many in the world are preoccupied with safety, and understandably so. We see that the one true God isn't safe. He is to be feared because of the intense holiness that characterizes his being, and thus no one can stand before him. All deserve to be judged, condemned, and punished. A similar question is asked in Psalm 15:1:

> O Lord, who shall sojourn in your tent?
>> Who shall dwell on your holy hill?

The mountain represents the place where humans meet with God, but the mountain is holy and awesome because the Lord dwells there. We find a similar expression in Psalm 24:3:

Who shall ascend the hill of the LORD?
    And who shall stand in his holy place?

The prophet Joel describes a locust plague that devasted Israel, and the plague isn't ascribed to chance but strikes Israel because of its sin. The day of the Lord hasn't been one of salvation but judgment. Hence, Joel asks,

The day of the LORD is great and very awesome;
    who can endure it? (Joel 2:11)

Nahum prophesies about the judgment that will come on Assyria, which was guilty of human-rights abuses that were horrific:

Who can stand before his indignation?
    Who can endure the heat of his anger?
His wrath is poured out like fire,
    and the rocks are broken into pieces by him. (Nah. 1:6)

These words aren't limited to Assyria, though they certainly apply to that country, but they apply to human beings generally. We might blithely say that we want the Lord to come and to make everything right without considering what that might mean for our own lives. Malachi poses the decisive question: "But who can endure the day of his coming, and who can stand when he appears? For he is like a refiner's fire and like fullers' soap" (Mal. 3:2). Malachi's words are played out in Jesus's ministry, as the religious leaders, although they didn't experience judgment immediately, could not stand in Jesus's presence. They were shown to be unholy. Revelation 6:12–17 anticipates the final judgment, the coming day of the Lord, the day when the one seated on the throne and the Lamb of God come to judge the world. That day is "the great day of their wrath," and the question is "Who can stand?" (Rev. 6:17).

The repetition of this same basic question illustrates the inadequacy, sin, and defilement of human beings. When we think of the judgment, if we don't belong to Christ we should not be filled with confidence but foreboding. How can we avoid the judgment since we share the same plight as all people everywhere, as those who have sinned against the Holy One of Israel?

The question asked at the conclusion of Revelation 6 ("The great day of [the wrath of God and the Lamb] has come, and who can stand?") is answered in Revelation 7. Those who can stand in God's presence are the 144,000, those who are sealed and protected from the wrath of God (Rev. 7:1–8). The identity of the 144,000 is debated, of course, and I have argued elsewhere that the number should be read symbolically to refer to all Christians.[1] Revelation 7:9–17 gives us another picture of the 144,000, but in this section they are described as an uncountable multitude. The same group is in view, but different pictures are used to describe them. Here we discover the fundamental reason that the 144,000 (the uncountable multitude) can withstand the day of wrath:

> Then one of the elders addressed me, saying, "Who are these, clothed in white robes, and from where have they come?" I said to him, "Sir, you know." And he said to me, "These are the ones coming out of the great tribulation. They have washed their robes and made them white in the blood of the Lamb." (Rev. 7:13–14)

No human being can stand before the one seated on the throne and the Lamb, except those who have been redeemed by the blood of Jesus. The blood of Jesus refers to his death since the shedding of one's blood brings death. Believers escape judgment through the redeeming death of Jesus, through his great sacrifice on their behalf. Hence, there isn't room for a sense of superiority over unbelievers because we don't stand based on our own virtue or merits. Instead, the wonder of being

---

1   Thomas R. Schreiner, *Revelation*, in *Hebrews–Revelation*, vol. 12 of *ESV Expository Commentary*, ed. Iain M. Duguid, James M. Hamilton Jr., and Jay Sklar (Wheaton, IL: Crossway, 2018), 622–23; Thomas R. Schreiner, *Revelation,* BECNT (Grand Rapids, MI: Baker Academic, 2023) 293–99.

purchased and freed and liberated from sin shines brighter, since it stands in contrast with what is deserved.

The Forgiveness of God

We find this same theme in Psalm 130. The following verses are instructive:

> If you, O Lord, should mark iniquities,
>   O Lord, who could stand?
> But with you there is forgiveness,
>   that you may be feared. (Ps. 130:3–4)

No one can stand on his or her own. No one is worthy—all have transgressed and violated God's commands. God's forgiveness stands out as inestimably precious, since he could rightly and justly keep a count of our iniquities. But the Lord is also forgiving, a God who extends his compassion to those who turn to him in repentance and faith. Psalm 130 concludes with an affirmation of the Lord's "steadfast love," the reality of abundant redemption, and the promise that

> he will redeem Israel
>   from all his iniquities. (Ps. 130:7–8)

When we read the Scriptures canonically, we see that abundant redemption has come about through the atoning death of Jesus Christ, through whom "we have redemption through his blood, the forgiveness of our trespasses, according to the riches of his grace" (Eph. 1:7). When we recognize that our God has extended mercy instead of justice, redeemed us instead of judged us, forgiven us instead of condemned us, then the joy of forgiveness captures our hearts. We might think that Psalm 130:4 would conclude that God's forgiveness would lead us to love him. And it is certainly true that the forgiveness of sins leads us to love our God more, but here we are told that forgiveness leads us to fear God. This means that forgiveness of sins isn't cheap and should never lead us to treat God casually, as if we are on the same level with him. Receiving forgiveness from the King of kings and Lord of lords, being absolved by the one "whom no one has ever seen or can see" (1 Tim. 6:16), sparks awe, reverence, and holy fear. We don't presume upon the one who forgives us but respond with a kind of trembling joy. Once again, the joy of forgiveness shines when we consider what we deserve.

Another fascinating text about the joy of forgiveness is Micah 7:8–20. The prophet, who is perhaps speaking on behalf of Israel, recognizes that he will endure the Lord's anger since he has sinned against him. Clearly, the judgment isn't the final judgment, since he is confident that the Lord will be his light (Mic. 7:8), that he will vindicate and save him (Mic. 7:9). The final word for Israel is communicated in Micah 7:18–19:

> Who is a God like you, pardoning iniquity
>   and passing over transgression
>   for the remnant of his inheritance?
> He does not retain his anger forever,
>   because he delights in steadfast love.
> He will again have compassion on us;
>   he will tread our iniquities underfoot.
> You will cast all our sins
>   into the depths of the sea.

Israel's vindication will only come because the Lord will forgive their sin and absolve them of their rebellion. No other god is comparable, no other god shows such compassion, and no other god finds delight in showing faithful love to his people. The wonder of God's forgiveness blazes forth, particularly because Israel has sunk so low and has no human hope for recovery. We find the same sentiment in Ezra 9:13: "You, our God, have punished us less than our iniquities deserved and have given us such a remnant as this." The words of Psalm 103:13 have become a reality:

> As a father shows compassion to his children,
>   so the LORD shows compassion to those who fear him.

One of the most important texts relative to God's forgiveness and justice is Romans 3:21–26. More extended treatments of it can be found elsewhere.[2] Paul's long argument in Romans 1:18–3:20 shows that all are sinners, all deserve judgment, and no one is qualified to stand in God's presence. Still, God's saving righteousness has now been manifested in Jesus Christ, and his apocalyptic and eschatological righteousness that has broken into history also fulfills Old Testament promises (Rom. 3:21). The saving righteousness of God is experienced by all who put their faith in Jesus, whether one is a Jew or a Gentile, male or female, slave or free (Rom. 3:22). Justification, being declared in the right before a holy God, is free because of the astonishing grace of God in Christ Jesus, who has ransomed believers through his blood (Rom. 3:24).

Jesus is the mercy seat, the place where forgiveness becomes a reality through his atoning death (Rom. 3:25). Remarkably, Jesus is the priest, the victim, and the place where atonement is secured. The word for mercy seat (*hilastērion*) also carries the implication of both expiation and propitiation. The mercy seat is the place where sins are expiated, wiped away, erased, forgiven. The mercy seat is also the place where God's wrath (cf. Rom. 1:18; 2:5; 3:5) is satisfied, appeased, propitiated. Through the death of Christ, then, the judging righteousness of God has been demonstrated (Rom. 3:25–26). God "passed over former sins" (Rom. 3:25), but he didn't overlook such sins as one who didn't care about justice and righteousness. The passing over of sins should not be misunderstood to say that God's forgiveness compromises his justice and holiness. Instead, he overlooked sins in his patience (Rom. 2:4) because he looked ahead (so to speak) to Christ's atoning sacrifice. At the cross, God manifested his judging and saving righteousness, and in doing so he was both "just" (*dikaion*) and "justifier" (*dikaiounta*) of those who put their trust in Jesus (Rom. 3:26). In showing mercy, he didn't compromise his justice, since Jesus took the place of sinners. As

---

2   For a recent treatment, see Brendan Byrne, *Paul and the Economy of Salvation: Reading from the Perspective of the Last Judgment* (Grand Rapids, MI: Baker Academic, 2021), 92–102; see also Thomas R. Schreiner, *Romans,* 2nd ed., BECNT (Grand Rapids, MI: Baker Academic, 2018), 502–5.

2 Corinthians 5:21 says, "He made him to be sin who knew no sin, so that in him we might become the righteousness of God." God placed our sin judicially on Christ, and thus his justice was vindicated. At the same time, he forgave the sins of those who turn to him for forgiveness so that believers experience God's saving righteousness and are credited with the righteousness of God in Christ.

The centrality of the cross is of supreme importance because it answers the question how God can forgive sins without compromising his righteousness and holiness. At the same time, it isn't the case that there is some *law* above God that he *has to abide by.* It isn't as if God wants to forgive sinners, but justice and the law stand in the way. Rather, holiness and justice aren't extrinsic to God but intrinsic to his very being and character. If he forgave sins apart from satisfying justice, it would be comparable to God lying, which is impossible since God can't lie (Num. 23:19). God can't do anything contrary to his character and still be God, for, as systematic theologians rightly say, God's essence can't be separated from his attributes. Nothing forces God to satisfy justice. Quite the contrary, God *is* justice and righteousness, and his very being defines what justice is. The cross is amazing because at the cross both the holiness and love of God are displayed, both his justice and mercy; he appeases his justice and forgives our sin as we trust in Jesus.

The Love of God

The love of God etched against the background of the justice of God stands forth with brilliance and splendor. God is not a passive and avuncular person who winks at sin and transgression, declaring that evil doesn't really matter and that all is well. Instead, wickedness is dealt with fully and finally at the cross, and forgiveness is extended to all who repent and believe. When one sees the love of God in the cross—the love of the Father in sending the Son, the love of the Son in being willing to give his life, and the love of the Spirit in applying the work of the Father and the Son to believers—the joy of our salvation leaps up afresh in our souls. We look at the cross and see the suffering of the Savior, and we realize what we deserved, recognizing that the love of God is a costly love. We think of Isaiah 66:24, which seems macabre at first glance: "And they shall go out and look on the dead bodies of the men who have rebelled against me. For their worm shall not die, their fire shall not be quenched, and they shall be an abhorrence to all flesh." The point of the text isn't exultation over the punishment of the wicked. Instead, the punishment of the wicked reminds believers of the destiny they deserve apart from God's grace, and such a state of affairs fills them with gratefulness for the fate they escaped, just as one trembles with joy after a car turns over in a wreck and one walks away uninjured.

Another text to consider is Romans 9:22–23. There are many difficulties in this famously controversial text that we will skip over, and I will assume the reading that I have defended elsewhere.[3] We see first in Romans 9:22 that God patiently endured those who are vessels of wrath, those who are destined for eschatological destruction. We might wonder why God patiently endures those whom he has decreed to destroy. This conundrum has been tackled in various ways in the history of interpretation. I suggest that we have a classic example of the mystery of divine sovereignty and human responsibility. God truly wants all to be saved and to come to the knowledge of the truth (1 Tim. 2:4; cf. Ezek. 18:32), and yet he hasn't decreed that all will do so. Human choices make a difference. They are authentic and real, and yet God has a script for history that will certainly be written since he "declar[es] the end from the beginning" (Isa. 46:10). As Job asserts, none of God's purposes "can be thwarted" (Job 42:2) since he is the one "who works all things according to the counsel of his will" (Eph. 1:11). No illustration works perfectly since we are talking about God, and his ways are above our ways. But God is like the author of a book who has written the story of every character, and yet the characters in the book make their own choices and are not mere puppets. Thus, God patiently waits for the wicked to repent and longs for them to repent, while at the same time he has ordained whatever comes to pass, even predetermining those

3 Schreiner, *Romans*, 505–11.

who won't repent. Many, of course, think talking like this is nonsense and contradictory, but it is better to hold onto every dimension of the biblical witness and to acknowledge that some truths are mysterious, far exceeding our ability to understand them.

Romans 9:23 informs us why—with a purpose clause—God wanted to display his wrath for those ordained for destruction. He did this, "in order to make known the riches of his glory for vessels of mercy, which he has prepared beforehand for glory." I take this to mean that the vessels of mercy, those who receive mercy and are saved, grasp more sharply and clearly the wonder of the mercy extended to them when they consider the destiny of those who experience God's wrath. A beautiful diamond stands forth in all its beauty against a black cloth. The warmth of the sunshine in the spring stands out in Minnesota in contrast to Florida since Minnesotans experience savagely cold winters. The warmth of the sun is glorious, delightful, and beautiful after experiencing a cold that penetrates to the bones. So, too, Paul's point is that God's mercy has a sharper profile when we consider the wrath we deserve. Perhaps that is one reason that angels long to grasp the salvation revealed in Christ (1 Pet. 1:12). The angels who sinned were not granted mercy, reminding us that mercy is truly undeserved. And the angels who stayed true to the Lord didn't need the mercy that we need as guilty sinners so that they can't fully grasp the mercy granted to us since they haven't experienced it. In any case, Paul in Romans 9 isn't inviting believers to rejoice over the destiny of the damned but to rejoice over the compassion and mercy they themselves received. Believers rejoice in God's mercy since they realize that they deserved wrath. We are more grateful and conscious of the blessing of health after a long sickness, and we praise God for his mercy when we feel, really feel, that we should have faced his wrath.

Conclusion

When we feel and sense that we deserve judgment, the beauty and loveliness of God's mercy stands forth in all its splendor. Forgiveness isn't cheap or trivial but precious and costly. In forgiving sinners God does

not compromise his justice. The justice of God is satisfied in the atoning sacrifice of his Son. As Jeremy Treat says, we should not conceive
of this as the Father punishing the Son since the Father always loves
the Son. Thus, Treat emphasizes Romans 8:3 where God condemns sin
in Christ's flesh. Treat says, "I think it would be more wise to say that
God in Christ bore our punishment because of his love."[4]

---

4   Jeremy Treat, *The Atonement: An Introduction*, SSST (Wheaton, IL: Crossway, 2023),
    51n27.

Epilogue

SOME MIGHT WONDER WHY we even need a *final* judgment since we are judged at our death for the lives we have lived. For instance, T. Desmond Alexander argues, in a careful article on Sheol, that Sheol is the place of confinement for the ungodly immediately after death, while the godly wait peacefully for the Lord to rescue them from death.[1] Not much is said in the New Testament about what happens to believers immediately after death in the intermediate state between our death and resurrection. The few hints we have, however, indicate that we are in God's presence. Jesus promises the repentant thief, "Today you will be with me in paradise" (Luke 23:43). Paul suggests that if he were to die he would immediately "be with Christ" (Phil. 1:23). Those who have died before the day of final judgment and the resurrection of the dead are "away from the body and at home with the Lord" (2 Cor. 5:8). The state of the wicked immediately after death isn't a subject of discussion in the New Testament, but some kind of verdict is presumably passed since they, in contrast to believers, are not present with the Lord in paradise.

Louis Berkhof answers concisely and convincingly why there is a final judgment, even if the destiny of human beings is fixed at death:

> [The final judgment] will serve the purpose . . . of displaying before all rational creatures the declarative glory of God in a formal, forensic

---

1 T. Desmond Alexander, "The Old Testament View of Life after Death," *Them* 11 (1986): 41–46.

act, which magnifies on the one hand His holiness and righteousness, and on the other hand, His grace and mercy. Moreover, it should be borne in mind that the judgment at the last day will differ from that at the death of each individual in more than one respect. It will not be secret, but public; it will not pertain to the soul only, but also to the body; it will not have reference to a single individual, but to all men.[2]

Berkhof's understanding can be summarized as follows:

Individual death	Final judgment
secret	public
soul	body and soul
single individual	all people

The final judgment declares to the world God's verdict on the lives of all people everywhere. In addition, the Scriptures clearly teach that life is incomplete until we are raised from the dead. Once we are raised, the fullness of life promised to us is realized.

I close this book by considering Psalm 58. David in this psalm reflects on the evil of human rulers, on the violence and evil perpetrated by them (Ps. 58:1–2). They are like venomous snakes full of poison and lying (Ps. 58:3–5). David asks God to judge them, to smash their teeth, to defang them, to deprive them of life (Ps. 58:6–8). He affirms that the wicked will be swept away (Ps. 58:9), but that raises a question for all of us. Who among us can say, "I am righteous and free from evil"? We know from the gospel of Jesus Christ that forgiveness is granted to all who turn from their sins and who put their faith in Jesus who died, "the righteous for the unrighteous, that he might bring us to God" (1 Pet. 3:18). God is both just and merciful, offering a way to escape the judgment that is coming. But for those who refuse to admit their sin, who harden their hearts against his love, who mistreat and

2   Louis Berkhof, *Systematic Theology*, 4th ed. (Grand Rapids, MI: Eerdmans, 1938), 731. Justin Taylor pointed me to Berkhof's comments and produced the accompanying chart.

discriminate against the righteous, judgment is coming. And those who are righteous by faith will rejoice when justice is done (Ps. 58:10). Believers will see that God is just and fair, that there is no impartiality or wickedness in him.

> Mankind will say, "Surely there is a reward for the righteous;
> surely there is a God who judges on earth." (Ps. 58:11)

General Index

Scripture and Ancient Sources Index

Also Available from Thomas R. Schreiner

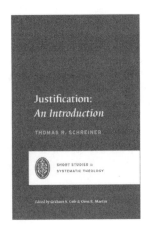

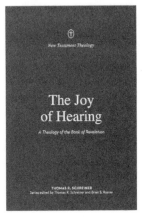

For more information, visit **crossway.org**.